Mindy

# Mindy

by Dorothy Hamilton

*Illustrated by Edwin B. Wallace*

HERALD PRESS
Scottdale, Pennsylvania
Kitchener, Ontario

Library of Congress Cataloging in Publication Data
Hamilton, Dorothy, 1906-
  Mindy.

  SUMMARY: Mindy strives to understand her position in
her parents' lives after their divorce and to adjust to
the loneliness of a new way of life.
  [1.  Divorce — Fiction] I. Wallace, Edwin B., illus.
II.  Title.
PZ7.H18136Mi                    [Fic]            72-5098
ISBN 0-8361-1692-5

MINDY

Copyright © 1973 by Herald Press, Scottdale, Pa. 15683
  Published simultaneously in Canada by Herald Press,
  Kitchener, Ont. N2G 1A7
Library of Congress Card Number: 72-5098
International Standard Book Number: 0-8361-1692-5
Printed in United States

Third Printing, 1975

Mindy

# 1

Sometimes Mindy Porter made a list of memories in her mind. She did this on days when she was especially homesick — like this June afternoon, three months after her parents' divorce.

She walked down the long hall of the apartment house and waited at the elevator. The whistling hum stopped at the fifth, then the fourth floor. No one else was waiting for the scrolled iron gates to open. "If there were I wouldn't know them," Mindy thought.

The air was warm and the sunshine probably as bright as it was in Oakville, twelve miles away. But here Mindy had to look straight up to see the cotton candy clouds. And the only trees were in wooden tubs outside Wellington Towers. Their tops were trimmed into strange shapes, round like leafy pom-poms and pointed like green triangles.

Mindy walked slowly along the street. She really didn't know where she was going. To the library, maybe? Or the park across and down the street? She couldn't go uptown without permission from her mother. *Anyway there's little money to spend.*

She'd thought of calling her mother at the Silver Brush. But Friday was the busiest day in the beauty shop and her mother had been cross when Mindy'd called the week before. "But I had to get permission. She would've been angrier if I hadn't asked if I could go to Oakville three hours ahead of time."

Mindy crossed over to the library and wandered around among the stacks of teenage books. But no title caught her interest. She kept remembering last weekend. Adding things to her list of memories of home.

First was the look on her father's face when the elevator doors parted with a clang. He was waiting and his gray eyes looked a little misty even when his face crinkled into a smile.

"Hi, Melinda Jane," he said. "Ready to go?"

"Am I ever!" Mindy said. "I'm glad you came early."

"Well, it was a case of necessity," her father said. "Coming early I mean. I had to pick up a couple items at the wholesale house before four o'clock. But I'd have waited. Any trouble getting away?"

"No," Mindy said, "not really." She didn't want to say that her mother had grumbled and brought

7

up the old rule that the judge set for visiting hours, from six o'clock on Friday evening until the same time on Saturday.

She didn't want to say that there wasn't much to do in the new place. This seemed strange to her, especially when she remembered all the things her mother had said about living in the city. She'd made it seem like an exciting adventure when she was trying to prepare Mindy for the divorce and leaving Oakville.

Mindy hadn't wanted to leave her home. She didn't understand divorce then any more than she did now. Wasn't a marriage a promise and what right did a judge or anyone have to break it? Again and again Mindy thought, "How about me? Should I just be passed around and divided up like the Westminster clock and the blue velvet settee and the inlaid coffee table?"

The same thought came to her mind as her father drove toward Oakville. So many hours with Daddy; a lot more with Mother. Passed around like — like a rented floor polisher or something.

She brushed her red-gold hair back over her shoulders and tried to erase sad thoughts. She felt like pushing on the floorboard to get home faster.

It wasn't the same without her mother. But it was better than the three-room apartment with the angular modern furniture, oyster white drapes, and bright red area rugs.

"What shall we have to eat tonight?" her father asked. "Or would you rather go to the drive-in?"

"I'd rather cook and stay at home *every single* minute," Mindy said.

"Fine with me," her father said. "We'll stop at the Jiffy Market. So get your thinking cap on."

After they turned off the state highway on to the Tarvia road, her father asked. "It isn't any better, is it, Mindy-girl?"

"No," Mindy said shaking her head. "Lately I've wondered, Why do kids have to go with their mothers?"

Jay Porter glanced sidewise at his daughter. Mindy could feel him looking at her. She stared straight ahead and blinked to keep tears back.

"Now honey, you know you love your mother," he said.

"Yes — but I love you too. And my home. Daddy, it's so lonely. Mom's gone all day and sometimes —" Then she stopped. It seemed a little disloyal to tell about her mother going out with Brad Northcutt. There probably wasn't anything really wrong about it. *But it would hurt Daddy even more than he already is. He's so thin.*

"Well, maybe it'll be better when school begins," her father said. "Then you'll make new friends."

A whole row of protests popped in her mind like a string of little firecrackers. She didn't want new friends. She didn't want to go to Wayne City High School. She just *had* to move back to Oakville before September.

They pulled up to the one grocery store in Oakville. Mindy looked around to see if any of her friends were in sight. She caught a glimpse of two girls on bicycles. They turned at the church corner and went south.

"Well, hop out," her father said. "Let's stock up on food."

*Mindy and her father*

Mindy bought chops because her father loved the way she cooked them with brown gravy. She included materials for a cheesecake and was looking at the fresh vegetables.

"Don't need to buy them," her father said. "We have green beans and leaf lettuce in the garden."

Somehow the thought of her father working in the garden made Mindy wonder, "Why is Daddy doing it now?" Her mother had been the gardener in the family. She'd raised all they could eat, also for freezing or canning, with plenty left to give away.

That was before she took the beautician's course. That's when things changed, when the quarrels — the serious ones — began.

After Lila passed her state exams things were better for a while. She wasn't so tired from studying at night and taking classes in the daytime. But after she went to work in the Silver Brush her family took second place.

At least that's how it seemed to Mindy. But she hadn't been unhappy. She was at home then, where she belonged, in the red brick house with the white shutters.

The house looked the same as they pulled up to the double doors of the garage. "Daddy's doing a good job of keeping it nice. I know why. He still thinks Mom will come back some day."

Mindy ran up to her room. A summer breeze blew the ruffled curtains inward. There was a cluster of pink rambler roses in a cut glass basket. She touched her maple chest and the hobnail bedspread and gave her small white rocker a shove with her foot.

"The house looks nice — like always. I'll have to call Aunt Eileen and tell her. Or run over if I have time." Mindy knew that her father's younger sister came over and cleaned once a week. Her aunt had said that she tried to get her father to eat meals with her.

Mindy looked at the hall clock as she ran downstairs. "After I get the cheesecake in the refrigerator and the chops in the oven I'll call Judy. Maybe she'll come over and help me make this house come alive for Daddy."

The next twenty-four hours were filled with familiar and pleasant happenings. They added to the list of memories in Mindy's mind. She wanted to hold on to every minute.

Judy came over and ate with Mindy and her father. She had a lot to tell about the summer swim lessons and her new quarter horse which was stabled at her grandfather's. She knew who was going to church camp and the schedule for tennis lessons.

Mindy wanted to hear all the news, but in a way it hurt to realize how much she was missing.

Judy cut off a chunk of cheesecake with her fork. "Say! I've been meaning to ask. How'd you get to be such a good cook? I burn TV dinners."

"You know," Mindy said. "I was in 4-H four years. And I had a lot of practice while Mother was in beauty school — and still do."

Mindy looked at her father. There were question marks in his eyes. *He's wondering how much Mother's gone. How much I'm alone. But he won't ask.*

It was different when she was with her mother. *I'll have to answer all kinds of questions when I get back. Like who did I see? Did anyone call Daddy? Is the house a mess?*

Judy helped do dishes and then the girls played croquet with Mr. Porter. He loved the game and had set up the wickets just in case anyone was in the notion of hitting a few balls.

The moon came up above the fringe of trees on the horizon. Fireflies flitted and glinted around the rose hedge. Wooden mallets hit round balls and the click-clacks were like music to Mindy.

After Judy left, Mr. Porter made lemonade from frozen concentrate while Mindy popped corn. Then they watched television until eleven o'clock.

As they went upstairs Mindy turned to flick the switch to put out the hall light. Her father bit his lip before he said, "I leave it on."

Mindy knew what he meant. They'd always left it on when someone was away. *He's waiting for someone to come back. It's times like this when I almost hate my mother.*

She stopped at the doorway of her room. "What time will you leave to go to the store?"

"I thought I'd stick around here until at least

14

ten," her father said. "We don't have much business before then. Joe Irwin can handle things."

Mindy knew he wanted to stay home because of her. There was always something to do at the store, especially since her father did a lot of the repair work.

"Well, call me," Mindy said. "And I'll go to the store with you."

"You don't have to," her father said.

"I know that," Mindy said. "But I wouldn't feel like I'd been home if I didn't."

He kissed her cheek and gave her hair a gentle tug. He started to speak then he smiled. "You already know I'm glad you're here, I guess."

"I know," Mindy said. "That makes two of us."

Mindy didn't go to sleep for a long time. She had to practically prop her eyelids up in order to stay awake. She wanted to soak up the familiar sounds and scents of home. Like the whisking of the honeysuckle vine against the side of the house and the fragrance of the cream-apricot blossoms. Mindy loved those flowers. They were like delicate trumpets.

She drifted into sleep and the next thing she heard was the clattering chuff of the power mower. She hurried to the window and saw her father criss-crossing the yard. The clean fragrance of mown grass filled the air. Her father called it invisible chlorophyll

Mindy made hot cakes while her father dressed to go to the store. They'd finished eating when the telephone rang. "Kip Sanders," Mindy's father said "It's for you — naturally."

"Hi," Mindy said.

"Hi yourself, stranger," Kip said. "You going to be

15

too busy for a game of tennis? I haven't beaten anyone since the last time you were home."

"Well, maybe I'd better squeeze you in," Mindy said. "If your ego needs rebuilding *that* badly."

Kip was fun. They'd never actually dated, just gone together in groups. Mindy's mother didn't think girls should go out on couple-dates until they were sixteen. Mindy hadn't felt rebellious or resentful about this until the last few months. Rules were OK. They sort of supported a person in her choice-making. Now one thought kept coming to mind. *Does Mom go by rules?*

After leaving the tennis court Mindy and Kip went to Polly's Place for cokes and pizza. Several Oakville classmates were in the booths and everyone was great. No one looked at her as if she were different or out of the group. No one asked questions. No one except Kip.

He didn't say anything until they were near her father's store. "Is it forever, Mindy?"

"You mean living in the city? Or the divorce?"

"Both or either," Kip said.

"I can't let myself believe that I'll not come back," Mindy said. "I hate it — the whole thing, Kip. It's so wrong."

"Do your parents know how you feel?"

"I've tried to tell Mom. But she doesn't seem to hear. Not really."

"And your dad?"

"I don't have to tell him," Mindy said. "We feel the same. I know we do."

"School sure won't be the same without you," Kip said.

16

"How about *me?*" Mindy asked. "I'll have all of you to miss. But I'm not going to think about that. I *have* to get back before September."

"But how? Didn't the judge say — "

"He said," Mindy answered. "But there's a lot he doesn't know. And neither do *I* — how, I mean."

"You'll be back next Saturday?" Kip asked.

"Yes. Of course. But it hurries Daddy to get me back between the time the store closes and the deadline."

As it turned out Mindy didn't get back until after six-thirty. There was a flurry of customers at closing time. He couldn't run them out. And they stopped at the Redwood Drive-in for breaded tenderloins and hot chocolate as planned.

In the fifteen-minute drive from the restaurant to the apartment Mindy said a lot more than she ever had to her father about the divorce. She hadn't planned it that way. It just came out, like music, when she put a needle on the record.

"Daddy," she began, "I don't think I can stand to live in Wayne City much longer. It's not fun like Mom said. It's lonely, cold, and scary and I can't bear to think of winter there."

"Wait a minute, Melinda — what do you mean scary?" her father asked.

"Oh, you know," Mindy said. "You hear the news. Stuff goes on in the streets and other places."

"In your building?" her father asked.

"We don't know for sure. But the police siren woke us up twice. I peeked out and saw the whirling red light."

"Were you alone?"

17

"No, not that time."

"But sometimes you are?" her father asked.

"Sometimes," Mindy said. "Mother always fixes it so I can stay with Callie — you know the operator in the next chair. But Callie talks on the phone a lot. I feel — well, in the way. Or out of place."

Her father pulled up to the curb and turned to grasp one of her wrists. "Promise me, Mindy, call me long distance the minute you feel afraid. Reverse the charges."

"I'd like to," Mindy said. "But what could you do from so far away?"

"I'd do something. Then and later."

"Oh, Daddy, you're so good to me."

"Well, what kind of a guy would I be if I weren't."

Lila Porter was pacing the floor when Mindy reached the apartment. "You're late," she said. "That's like Jay. Coming early, bringing you back late. I don't know what — "

"Please, Mother. Please don't spoil things. It's been so great."

Her mother's face reddened down to her neck. For a minute Mindy thought she was going to keep on scolding. Then her face sort of crumpled. Like she was about ready to cry.

"I'm sorry, Mindy. I'm awfully tired. My last customer was finicky."

"Are you going someplace?" Mindy asked.

"No. Not really. Just down to Callie's. You're invited."

Mindy shook her head. "I'd rather not."

"Why?"

"Oh, Mother. You and Callie make me feel so

*Mindy's mother, Lila*

left out, talking about stuff that makes me uncomfortable."

"You mean Brad," her mother said. "You don't think I should go out with him? I can tell."

Mindy brushed her hair back over her shoulders and started toward the bedroom. What could she say? She *didn't* like Brad. Or the divorce. Or living in the city. Or thinking of her daddy being alone. But what good would talking do? It'd take something else to change things.

# 3

Mindy's mother made a special effort to fill Sunday with fun. In fact it seemed that she strained to make every free minute full of excitement, to be on the go all the time.

Sometimes Mindy thought, "Talk about teenagers, Mom and Callie can outdo anyone my age. At least they try."

Brad Northcutt was out of the city for a few days. That was a plus for Mindy. She wouldn't be left alone or parked at Callie's or coaxed or forced to go along.

Mindy was awake for a long time before her mother got up. She'd brought two favorite books back from Oakville. Mindy tiptoed into the living room to get them. Her mother was asleep on the sofa bed. She wouldn't take the one bedroom for herself, saying Mindy needed more sleep. "Besides, when I have company you'd be kept up late." Company usually meant Brad.

As she turned to go back to the bedroom, Mindy's eyes centered on her spinet piano. It looked out of place. Fruitwood didn't match plastic and splashy colors.

Mindy wished she could sit down and play a while. She didn't think she was such a great musician or anything professional, but she'd taken lessons for four years and been in the advanced student recital for half of that time.

She'd played more than ever since they'd moved to Wayne City. She couldn't take lessons because there wasn't enough money even if her mother had time to find a good teacher.

She'd played to fill the hours. She'd played to erase loneliness. She could shut her eyes and pretend she was at home and that she could see the rose corduroy couch in front of the fireplace. And hear the whirr of the golden balls of the Westminster clock on the mantel.

She'd turn the book's pages fifty times before her mother came to the door. She looked rested and pretty — more like she used to. Her hair wasn't lacquered in place yet. Little curls edged her forehead.

"Hungry?" she asked.

"Yes," Mindy said. "But I can cook. I didn't want to wake you."

22

*Mindy at the piano*

"No. No," Lila Porter said. "You do more than your share of cooking around here as it is. What would you like? Hot cakes?"

"Well, Mindy said, "I had them yesterday."

Her mother picked up a can of spray and a minosa-scented mist settled on her hair. "I suppose you had to cook out there, too."

"Some of the time," Mindy said. "But I wanted to. Daddy's so — " Then she stopped. *Why tell her? She doesn't care.*

"So, what?" her mother said. "Thin? Maybe that's his own fault. Maybe he just wants the whole town to think he's a martyr."

Mindy felt warm tears in her eyes. Nothing was as hard to bear as this bitterness. Was this one of the reasons she was happier in Oakville? Her father never said an unkind word about her mother.

"I shouldn't have said that. No matter how I think," her mother said. "I have no right to whittle away at what you think of your father."

"You can't," Mindy said softly.

"But he can at *me*!"

"He never does, Mom. Never."

Lila started to say something then turned and walked toward the kitchen. Within a few minutes she called Mindy to eat scrambled eggs and toast.

Later they rode across town to the university and visited the arboretum, the greenhouses, and the botanical gardens. Once Mindy started to tell about the green vegetables her father was growing and that the lavender rose was in bloom. *But she doesn't care. She wanted to leave all that.*

They ate at The Inn near the bus stop. Her

24

mother watched the group of summer students. "They're so alive," she said. "So young and vibrant."

Mindy studied the faces of several university people. "Some look sad to me. Sort of lost or bewildered," she said.

"Would you like to go to a movie?" her mother asked as they rode back toward the apartment.

"No. Not really," Mindy said. "I brought some music from home. And besides nothing good is on. I'd rather watch TV."

Her mother didn't say anything until they were in the elevator. "Oakville is still home to you, I guess."

"Yes. It is."

While Mindy played and wrote letters her mother talked to Callie on the telephone, went to the drugstore for a magazine which she leafed through but didn't read, and paced the floor. She seemed more restless all the time.

At four-thirty the door buzzer rang. Mindy opened it and saw Judy and her parents.

"Well, hi," she said. "Come on in."

"Didn't know I was coming to return your visit so soon, did you?" Judy said.

"No. But I'm glad," Mindy said. "Mother! Company."

Lila Porter came out of the bedroom smiling, but not with her eyes. The Porter and Rayburn families had been friends as well as neighbors. They'd shared cookouts and homemade ice cream and family movies.

There'd been a break in the relationship when Lila began to talk to Martha Rayburn about a divorce. Or was it when Martha tried to change Lila's mind?

Mindy was surprised that the Rayburns came. She

could tell that her mother wasn't pleased. *Maybe she thinks they're here to try to talk her into coming back. Maybe they did.*

"Why don't I fix us some iced tea or lemonade?" Mindy's mother said.

"Oh, no. Not yet," Martha said. "We just stopped at an orange crush stand in the Mall."

No one except the girls seemed to know what to say. Judy was bubbling over with plans for the ice-cream social to be held on the church lawn in two weeks. "And you're on a committee, Mindy. Rev. Carmondy read your name."

"But I don't get to go to church," Mindy said. "And I always have to be back here by six."

"They'll begin serving at four," Judy said. "You could get in on *some* of the fun."

"That's one reason we stopped by," Martha Rayburn said. "We are on the way home from my mother's. We'd love to have Mindy stay at our house that Saturday night, if that would suit you."

"Well, I don't know," Lila said. "Once I begin making exceptions to the ruling — "

"But if you lived in Oakville the girls would be staying overnight with each other," Martha said.

"I guess you're right," Mindy's mother said. "And we'd like for Judy to visit us here."

The girls smiled and exchanged winks. Then Mindy asked Judy to take a walk. "There's not so much to see today. The library's closed. But sometimes there's a band concert in the park."

"Don't be long," Mr. Rayburn said. "We should head home by a quarter before six if we want to get to church on time."

After the Rayburns left Mindy noticed that her mother was unusually quiet. She sat on the end of the couch and sipped iced tea now and then. She made one glass last for nearly an hour. What had happened? Had the Rayburns said something to upset her? She didn't seem angry. Just thoughtful. What could have quieted her restlessness? Mindy hoped it would last.

Callie came to the apartment and for a change Mindy wasn't uneasy. Her mother made toasted cheese sandwiches and served ice cream. She kept the conversation on hairstyles, makeup, and fashions. Brad's name wasn't mentioned — not once.

After Callie left and as Mindy turned to go to her room she said, "Mother, thanks for saying I could stay with Judy."

"Well, I'm not *always* a grouch," her mother answered. "Besides, it may work out for the best. Brad said something about going to a regatta that Saturday."

"So that's it," Mindy thought. "It'd be handier for her and Brad if I was out of the way."

"But I may not go," her mother said. "It all depends."

*On what?* Mindy was afraid to ask.

# 4

After the excitement of the weekend, the apartment seemed even lonelier. Mindy didn't know what to do.

Lila Porter was one of the few Silver Brush operators who took appointments on Monday. The others either attended classes, shopped, or caught up on their housework.

Mindy knew her mother was willing to work because she needed more money. "But why?" she often thought. "I know Daddy offered to sell the house and give her what it brought above the mortgage. He'd have let us live there if Mom hadn't been determined to work in the fancy salon and move to the city."

When her mother finished her beauty course she'd worked in Ruby Wheeler's two-chair shop in Oakville. Things went well until Callie came into the picture. She and Lila took Monday classes together and that's when Mindy began to hear snatches of quarrels between her parents.

Even if they did manage to keep her from hearing the arguments, they couldn't hide the results. Neither talked to the other at the table. Her father worked longer hours at the store. And her mother made long-distance calls to Callie almost every night. The big telephone bills brought on more than one quarrel.

Mindy hadn't liked the strained feelings but she didn't really worry about them. The idea of her parents getting a divorce had never occurred to her. One Monday night her mother didn't get home from class until one o'clock. Closed doors couldn't shut out the loud and angry talk that night. In that conversation the words sue, divorce, and incompatible were repeated several times.

The next few weeks were like a frightening dream to Mindy. She couldn't bear to look back on them even yet. Going through them was almost unbearable. Remembering hurt. But as time went on, three questions seemed to run through Mindy's mind like sad and minor chords in music. "Why? What happened? What can I count on now?"

The same refrain echoed in her thoughts after her mother left for her Monday appointments — two frostings, a permanent wave, and four shampoos — a full day's work.

Again Mindy began making lists in her mind to blot

out the unanswered questions. "It's like a tape recorder," she thought. "You put one thing on to erase another. But it doesn't erase completely. I can still hear echoes."

She decided to clean the rug in the apartment. Whoever'd lived there before had left their traces. As she brushed whirlpools of foamy suds into the red nap she wondered again, "Why didn't Mom want to bring anything from home? She loved our furniture and took such great care of it until she went to work. And why suddenly did she get this career idea?" One question seemed to lead to another and there were no answers, at least not as far as Mindy could see.

She decided to take a walk while the rug dried. She moved aimlessly, not knowing where to go or having any friends to meet. She met two boys at the corner. One whistled and the other said, "Hi, Babe!" Mindy pretended not to hear. She'd never be a pickup. *But it'd be easy. Because I'm lonely.*

The park which covered a square block was only a few trees, several green slatted benches, and two water fountains. It wasn't a playground, just a place to sit and walk. Mindy crossed to the other side on the winding walks for the first time. "There's a church! I've never seen it before."

For some reason she crossed the street and walked up the steps to the white frame building. The double doors were unlocked. One was propped open a few inches. Mindy heard singing, children's voices. Was it a choir? Then she caught a glimpse of a sign in the church yard. *Daily Vacation Bible School.* She'd gone to these in Oakville until she was twelve and been a helper every year since — until this one.

Mindy was tempted to go in. "But I don't belong. I *could* start to go to church here. But in a way that would be giving up — breaking with home."

As she headed toward the library she admitted to herself that her loneliness was partly her fault. She'd insisted that she be allowed to finish the school year at home. "Mom said even a few weeks here would help me make friends. And maybe staying at home *did* postpone making adjustments. It's like I'm here and my roots are in Oakville."

She stayed in the library until she suddenly felt hungry and realized she'd forgotten all about lunch. After checking out four books she hurried back to the Wellington Arms building.

A lady in a lovely flowered dress, pink, lavendar and mint, was waiting for the elevator. She was carrying a tiny dog — some kind of a poodle. Its hair was almost exactly the shade of the tint Callie used. Sort of a frosted ash-blond.

Mindy smiled at the lady as the dog yipped at her. "I guess it doesn't like strangers."

The dog's owner stared and twisted the jeweled collar round and round on her pet's neck. She didn't say a word.

*That pup's not the only person here that doesn't like strangers.*

Mindy made a lettuce, mayonnaise and tomato sandwich and sprinkled chives over cottage cheese. The telephone rang as she carried her tray toward the television.

"Mindy?" her Aunt Eileen's voice said, "I began to think I couldn't reach you until it was too late."

31

"Too late for what?" Mindy asked.

"Well, we're coming into town, Sharon and I. The 4-H Club Swim is next week and she's outgrown her suit by at least four inches. Want to go shopping with us?"

"Do I!" Mindy said. "At least I want to go. I probably won't buy anything."

"Don't be too sure. Your daddy ate here at noon. He gave me some splurging money for you."

"Great," Mindy said. "Will you come by here?"

"Why not?" her aunt said. "Listen for three beeps in about an hour."

"I'll be at the curb waiting," Mindy said.

After she hung up she realized that she should tell her mother where she was going. Or should she have asked?

She dialed the Silver Brush number and began choosing her words. Callie answered and said her mother was in the middle of a frost job. "Any message?"

"Yes," Mindy said. "Tell her I'm going uptown. And I'll be careful."

As she dressed in her green checked shift and white sandals she thought, "Mom wouldn't care if I went uptown alone — but she may not like it because I'm going with Aunt Eileen. Six months ago it would've been OK. But now — well I'm supposed all at once to be divorced from my dad's relatives."

The afternoon went quickly. Sharon was only twelve but she and Mindy had always been friends as well as cousins. After the lemon yellow swimsuit was purchased, Mindy went to the fabric and needlework departments. She bought some white powder puff muslin and some embroidery thread with some of the five dollars her father sent.

"I'm going to make a blouse and put Swedish embroidery around the yoke. It'll give me something to do."

Her aunt looked at her, then reached over and patted her cheek. "But you don't have a sewing machine in town."

"I know," Mindy said. "But I can cut it out and stitch the seams at home Saturday."

"Let me take your material and pattern," her aunt said. "I'll snip and sew and mail it in tomorrow. Or should I keep it until the weekend?"

"I'd rather you mailed it," Mindy said. "The days can be a week long here. They're not all like today. This has been special."

# 5

The next ten days didn't drag quite so slowly. Mindy had her blouse to work on, the day at home, and the bright prospect of being in Oakville for a whole weekend.

Her mother went out with Brad once in the middle of the week. Callie was away that night and Lila wanted to call Mrs. Andrews the apartment house manager to come up and stay with Mindy.

"I'd rather be alone," Mindy said. "I'd feel like I had to be polite and talk and it's a strain."

Her mother was pressing the dress she was going to wear that night, a navy linen with red and white accents. She set the iron down on the metal stand with a clang. "Are you *trying* to make me feel guilty?" she asked.

Mindy didn't answer for a while. She didn't know what to say at first. Then when she unraveled the answer from the knots in her thinking she was afraid to say what she really thought.

She kept on with what she was doing, working cardinal red floss into the stenciled outline of a tiny bird. Her mother picked up the hissing iron and edged it around the scalloped collar. She drew a deep breath and said, "You didn't answer."

"I know," Mindy said. "Because you won't like it. But, well, feeling guilty or not is up to you, isn't it?"

"I suppose so," her mother said. "But all the time I get this feeling. That you're blaming *me* for the divorce. That you are unhappy about it."

"I am. You should *see*."

"Well I guess I do. But I tried to make you understand."

Mindy put her sewing in her lap and looked straight at her mother's face. "Maybe understanding's like feeling guilty. It has to be *in* me. You *told* me what I *should* see. And how *you* felt. But I still don't see a good reason for making so many people unhappy. I just don't, Mom."

Her mother whipped the dress off the ironing board and said the same thing she'd said dozens of times before. "How about *my* happiness? Don't I have a right to some?"

This didn't make much sense to Mindy. It was like a wrong note in a musical chord.

She didn't say a word. It wouldn't do any good. Her mother had flounced to the bedroom. As

35

Mindy threaded the needle with deep green thread, thoughts echoed in her mind. "I know Mom's not *always* been unhappy. I don't think she's so joy filled now. I still don't know what's really wrong or see that Daddy's done anything so terrible."

She worked on her blouse until nearly nine o'clock. *Maybe I'll get it done to wear home.* She quit when the thread began to knot and she realized she was tired.

She fixed a glass of lemonade and spread crackers with peanut butter and took her snack to the couch. While waiting for the television to warm up she turned off the window fan. It clattered a lot. *And maybe the air's cooler now.*

She began to feel drowsy before the half-hour musical was over. Yet for some reason she didn't want to go to bed. If she'd been in Oakville she'd have called Judy or sat on the patio or maybe played a game of croquet with her father in the light of the backyard lanterns.

She turned off the television and picked up a book. "I'd rather play the piano but it's on the wall next to Mr. Stiffler. He complains that vibrations come through."

The book caught her in the movement of the Indian girl's story and she was far away on the wall of the Grand Canyon when she heard steps in the hall, loud steps which sort of stumbled. Mindy's heart seemed to throb in her throat.

She thought of what her father said. "Call me if you're afraid." She wanted to do that right now. But she wasn't sure there was any danger. Someone might just be trying to find his way home.

But Mindy was scared. She knew that people drank more than they should. She'd been taught that any was too much. She'd never been face-to-face with anyone who could not control his actions.

In fact she remembered hearing her mother tell Brad that she wouldn't go to a bar or cocktail party with him. Mindy felt good that she hadn't changed in *that* way.

Brad had started to laugh, sort of making fun of her mother. Evidently he saw that Lila was serious and said, "We'll see. Time and the city and I may change that small-town notion."

"Don't count on it," Lila said.

The footsteps were coming closer. Mindy held her breath. Then she heard nothing. Had whoever it was gone on? Or was it the man who lived across the hall?

Then she heard a squeak and a click. The doorknob was turning. She could see it moving. Her thoughts circled in high speed. Should I call Daddy? But he'd be frightened. Is it right to upset him if I can do something else? But what? Who can I call?

Without really coming to a clear decision she reached for the telephone and dialed the landlady's apartment. "Mrs. Andrews," she said softly almost in a whisper. "This is Mindy Porter. I think there's someone at my door."

"Is that where *he* is?" the lady said. Then her voice faded. But Mindy could hear her faintly, "Officer, he's on the third floor. Near 317."

Mrs. Andrews turned back and told Mindy that someone had robbed the movie two blocks over and that a thorough search was going on all over the area. "Are you scared, honey?" she asked.

"Yes, I am," Mindy said.

"Well, I don't blame you. So am I," Mrs. Andrews said. "I tell you what. I'll bring my knitting up and sit till your mamma gets back. We'll keep each other company."

Mindy heard other footsteps come down the hall. Then there was a scuffle and a muffled conversation. Mrs. Andrews came up within a few minutes and said that the intruder was the thief.

Mindy made hot chocolate for herself and the landlady. Her hands quit trembling before the foamy beverage was gone. She wished she could call her father. Just to hear his voice. *But that would be selfish. To worry him so I could feel better.*

Mrs. Andrews insisted that Mindy go on to bed. "I'll curl up here on the couch cozy as can be."

"You can turn on the TV," Mindy said. "It won't bother me."

"Well, I might as well," Mrs. Andrews said. "My set's been on the blink. Seems like it's taking forever to find out what's ailing it."

Mindy went to sleep but her dreams kept her on the edge of being awake. Then she heard her mother come in and talk to Mrs. Andrews. Then she came to the door. "Are you awake, Melinda?" she asked.

"Yes."

Her mother walked over and sat down on the edge of the bed. "I'm sorry, honey, I know how scared you must have been. Things like this go on everywhere. That's why we have a chain and bolt on the door."

"But not in Oakville," Mindy thought.

"That was good thinking," Mindy's mother said. "Calling Mrs. Andrews."

"I wanted to call Daddy," Mindy said. The words seemed to slip out. The feeling behind them had been strong for over two hours.

"Why?" her mother said. "Why did you think of calling *him*?"

"Because," Mindy said. "I knew where he'd be. And besides he told me that I should — whenever I was scared."

"You've been afraid here before?"

"Well, sure — weren't you?" Mindy asked. "When we heard the sirens in the night?"

"Yes, I was," her mother said. "But as I said this goes on. Millions of people live with it. Get used — " Then she stopped and got up. She walked to the window and came back and sat on the foot of the bed. She grasped one of Mindy's ankles and squeezed it.

"I'm not facing the facts, am I? Fifteen-year-old girls shouldn't be left alone so much where danger exists. And I'm the cause — you being alone is the result. I didn't foresee all this when I took it in my head to — "

"To what?" Mindy asked.

"I guess I'm not ready to talk about that, Mindy. I've got some more thinking to do. Anyway it's late. But *this* will not happen again."

# 6

By Friday evening the incident in the hall had faded to the back of Mindy's mind. She didn't say anything about it to her father.

The night and day in Oakville was a busy time as usual. She and her father went out to the farm to see her grandparents who had postponed their supper hour until seven.

Gram Porter had made puffy baked dumplings to eat with creamed chicken. They were like crusty pillows. As Mindy poured silver-flicked lemonade into tall cut glass tumblers she asked, "What you doing now? What's your summer project?"

Her grandmother smiled as she sliced butter over

the mound of mashed potatoes. "You know me, don't you, Mindy-girl? I'm always up to something."

"I think it's great," Mindy said. "No wonder you're so young!"

"Maybe so," Mrs. Porter said. "I just haven't stopped to let old age catch up with me."

"But you didn't tell me — what *is* new?"

"I'll show and tell after we eat," her grandmother said. "You call the men. But before you do — I was just thinking. Why couldn't you and your daddy sleep here? I'd get you up in time to open the store. How does that sound to you?"

"It hits exactly the right note," Mindy said. "I'm vibrating."

"Well, good. It'd be nice to think someone was upstairs. To hear footsteps in the hall."

A little daylight was left when the evening meal was over. Mindy and her father walked around the yard and barn. They stopped at the lot where the two Arabian horses grazed. "Do you still ride them every day, Granddad?"

"Yep. Unless the weather's too bad. Want me to saddle up?"

"We can do it for ourselves," Mindy's father said.

They took a short ride on the gravel road, down to the state highway and back. Mindy liked to hear the clicking-clurping of the hooves. And once in a while she saw little sparks fly when the iron horseshoes hit a stone.

The men watched television in between snatches of conversation about the Vietnam war and the slumping economy and the coming election. Mindy could hear them from her grandmother's bedroom. *It's*

41

*just like it used to be. Except Mom's not here.*

Mrs. Porter had pulled a tall cardboard carton out of her closet. "Turn that light on over the dressing table," she said. "I want you to get a good look. One of these is yours if you want it."

She began to lift straw bags out of the box and line them up on the bed.

Mindy picked up the first one. A velvet snail was perched in some green grass fringe and a cluster of pearl peas rested in lustrous pods. "Gram! these are great!! You made them?"

"I certainly did. I sort of let my imagination run wild, I guess."

Mindy ran a finger over plump velvet strawberries on one bag, soft purple grapes on another, and the gray and brown owls of another design.

"What are you going to do with all these?" she asked.

"Well, I'm selling some to the Meadowlark Gift Shoppe in the city and I'll give some away," her grandmother said. "To you and Sharon and your aunt — and to Lila — if she'd want one — from me."

Mindy looked up and saw a glisten in her grandmother's violet eyes. Without thinking she walked over and shut the door to the living room. "Gram, I have to ask you," she said. "It's like an ache in me. Do *you* know why my mother wanted a divorce?"

Her grandmother sank down on her wicker sewing rocker. "You don't? No, I don't suppose you do. I doubt if Lila does. Or if she'd admit or come right out and say."

"I don't understand," Mindy said.

"How could you?" Mrs. Porter said. "You've never

42

been your mother's age and she's never been mine looking back on the threshold."

"The threshold," Mindy was getting even more puzzled.

"I'll try to make myself clear. You curl up on the bed. There comes a time when a person realizes that the years are flying by at a more rapid rate than ever before. It can be scary. And folks do a lot of things to try to slow them down."

"You're saying that Mom doesn't want to get old?"

"I'm saying that Lila's more panicky than most women," her grandmother said. "Because of her mother."

Mindy remembered her Grandmother Staley. She'd been a person who'd enjoyed poor health, liking to have people wait on her, complaining to get sympathy. Mindy hadn't really liked to visit her. The house always smelled of camphor and the shades were down a lot, giving the rooms a gloomy look and a musty smell.

"I remember that Gram Staley always looked the same — no older," Mindy said. "Nor younger either."

Mrs. Porter said that Lila's mother had given up coping with life and responsibility. It seemed easier to her to live in a kind of medicated state.

"But what has that to do with Mom?" Mindy asked.

"Nothing really," her grandmother said. "Except in Lila's mind. Which is where all of us live." She went on to say that Lila Staley Porter looked almost exactly like her mother and that people had probably said this hundreds of times.

43

"I've thought all through this unhappy time that Lila's fighting to keep from being like Marda Staley. In fact, I *think* that's where the urge to go into beauty school sprouted."

Mindy wrinkled her forehead and thought about that sentence. "That makes sense," she said. "There's a lot of keeping-young stuff for sale in *The Silver Brush*. But why did it have to lead to divorce? What did *Daddy* do?"

Her grandmother sighed. "It's hard for me naturally — since I'm his mother — to see that your father did anything — except let Lila have her way. I just can't see though how she could do so much hurt. It really isn't like her."

"I know," Mindy said. "I've thought the same thing."

"Well, let's change the subject," Mrs. Porter said. "Find a way to cheer us up."

"I'm willing," Mindy said. "But first, thank you, Gram."

"For what?"

"For helping me understand a little better."

"Oh, Mindy-girl, I wish I could do more to make all of you happy."

Mindy ran to the chair and knelt down. "I know," she said as she leaned her head on her grandmother's shoulder. "I *feel* you loving me. I always have."

The four Porters stayed up until after the eleven o'clock news. Mindy's grandfather said, "It'd be a shame to waste all this sociability. I can sleep later."

They ate strawberry pie and ice cream and Mindy played a game of double nine dominoes with her father, then with his father.

After she went to bed she tried to put the puzzle of the divorce together. She had one more piece in place — the one about her mother not wanting to get old. But where did her father fit?

The sounds of the night were like soft music. Birds still twittered in the wild grapevines which climbed nearly to the top of the tapered tower of the windmill at the back gate. A soft breeze bumped against the screen wire which covered the long window. It was like a muffled drumbeat.

Mindy felt safe. The puffy featherbed was around her like a soft and sheltering nest. The sweetness of lilac sachet came from the crisp sheets.

She thought of the apartment — of the noise, the clacking of the faulty air conditioning, the traffic, and the loneliness.

*Be glad for now, Mindy Porter. Don't spoil it by thinking about the tomorrows.*

7

Mindy filled Saturday with the kind of activity which had seemed good to her for as long as she could remember. After her father went uptown to open the store she baked butterscotch brownies and put a casserole of cheese and potatoes in the oven. "There'll be enough for noon and night," she thought as she washed the dishes and scoured the sink.

While the oven did its work she called Judy and they planned to go for a swim at one. "And I'm supposed to tell you," Judy said. "Our committee meets at two for the ice-cream social."

Mindy went to the store at eleven so she could

*Mindy baked butterscotch brownies*

walk home with her father and to be with him as much as she could.

She wondered if she would see Kip on the way. He hadn't called. *But we weren't at home long last night.* She wondered if he was on the same committee.

Then it occurred to her that Kip could be interested in some other girl by now. He could have decided that he'd rather not wait around on someone who was in town only twenty-four hours a week. *I guess that's natural. And I shouldn't blame him.*

Judy came on her bike at 12:45. Mindy had just finished doing the lunch dishes. "Ready?" Judy called from the side door.

"Almost," Mindy answered. "Come on in."

"It's really hot," Judy said. "I'm *ready* for a swim. Shall we ride or walk? Or did you take your wheels to the city?"

"No, they're here," Mindy said. "It'd be no fun riding alone."

"Don't you know *anyone?*" Judy asked.

"No kids," Mindy said. "Oh, I see some, like in the library or the elevator or at the park. But no one speaks. And I'm a little scared — you know — maybe it wouldn't be safe."

"Don't any of your mother's new friends have children?" Judy asked.

"Not my age," Mindy said. She suddenly realized that Callie and most of the other operators, those who came to the apartment, were a lot younger than her mother. *So is Brad — even if Mom doesn't want to talk about that.*

"Well, I guess I'd feel the same way," Judy said. "But I'd also be terribly lonely."

48

"You think I'm *not?*"

As they rode up to the gate of the pool Mindy found out why she hadn't seen or heard from Kip. Judy had a message. "He's working in the tomato fields for his uncle. He said to tell you that if he doesn't get back to Oakville before you leave he'll see you next weekend."

Mindy knew that she'd not see him for another week unless it rained. She'd seen trucks filled with hampers of tomatoes lined up at the canning factory as they came in from the farm.

The hour at the pool was like a reunion. At least half of Judy's class was there, besides her cousin Sharon and other friends of various ages.

And the committee meeting was just as pleasant. Rev. Carmondy took the seven young people out on the red brick patio at the back of the parsonage. His pretty wife served sugary ginger cookies and frosty lemonade.

After the plans were made everyone got up to leave. Mindy felt that the minister was watching her. She could tell even if the sun was reflecting from his amber framed spectacles. As she started to follow Judy around the house he said, "It's good to know you'll be here all of next weekend, Melinda."

"It's good for me too," she said. Then without stopping to decide if she should or shouldn't she asked, "Do you have time to talk to me, Sir?"

"Certainly," the young minister said.

Mindy hurried to catch up with Judy and then came back.

"Sit down," the minister said. "And tell me what's on your mind."

"You probably already know," Mindy said as she perched on the edge of a wooden lawn chair. "The divorce."

Rev. Carmondy took off his glasses and began polishing them with a blue bordered handkerchief. "You are correct. I did know."

"Do you think they're right," Mindy asked. "Divorces, I mean."

"That's a question that puzzles a lot of people. I think I can only answer it, in individual cases, at least by looking at the results. So many times no one is happier. And too many are hurt."

Mindy felt tears in her eyes and running down her cheeks. No sobs, just tears. The minister didn't speak and neither did she until the tightness in her throat was almost gone. She could talk around it.

"That's the way it seems to me — with us. No one's happier."

"Not even your mother?"

"No," Mindy said. "She tries to act gay and lively. But — well, she's restless and has to work awfully hard."

"I can see that she would," the minister said. "Lila's attitude toward taking money from your father is the one hope I've had that there *might* be a reconciliation some day."

"Do you really think there might be? Why?" Mindy asked.

"Now, don't build up too much hope. But I sincerely feel that your mother's basic goodness and stronger values will eventually take over." He went on to say that Lila Porter *had* talked to him, even

50

though she hadn't taken his advice to move slowly. She'd said that she wouldn't ask for a division of property or alimony because her husband's business was just getting established. She'd felt that since *she* was the one who wanted to leave Oakville it wouldn't be fair to insist that the home be sold.

"So you see, Mindy, your mother wasn't unfair in all respects. Nor completely inconsiderate. Your father has made a private agreement on a later settlement."

The thought of talking to the minister about her mother's dread of being old came to Mindy's mind. But it seemed so personal. *I'd feel disloyal.*

"Well, I'd better go," she said. "And thank you for your time."

She hurried home to pack her overnight bag and get to the store to meet her father. She took a walk through the house to fill her mind with the feel of home. The telephone rang as she started downstairs.

Her father was calling. "I got to thinking," he said. "There are green beans going to waste in the garden and those squash your mother likes — or liked. What's the name of them?"

"Zucchini," Mindy said.

"Would you want to pick some?" her father asked.

"Sure," Mindy said. "They'll taste good."

"And Mindy — " her father added. "That rose-bush, the one we gave Lila for her birthday one time, is loaded. You know which one?"

"I know," Mindy said. "The lavender. The one which cost seven dollars and fifty cents and Mom said we were extravagant to buy. I'll clip a bouquet."

As she wrapped the prickly rose stems in wet newspapers she wondered how her mother would look when she saw them. Would she be angry?

On the way to the city Mindy's father talked more cheerfully than usual. He always tried to *act* happy. But his eyes and voice were often sad and strained. He talked about his business and the boom in tape players. He told that he'd taken on the volunteer job of teaching radio and TV repair to boys in the Correction Institute over in Wabash County. "I go two evenings a week," he said. "And I think it's helping the boys — and it's a way of filling time."

Mindy had to fight from crying when she left him at the elevator. Her arms were full of roses, vegetables, and luggage. And her heart was over-flowing with feelings of love."

"Don't cry, Mindy-girl," her father said. "Remember next week's visit will be twice as long."

As the elevator jerked to a stop Mindy had a kind of desperate feeling. If Mom's not there, I'm going to yell out the window to stop Daddy and go home with him."

She really didn't see that she'd be so wrong. "If Mom's where she wants to be and that's not with me or where I'd rather stay, what sense does all this loneliness make?"

Before she reached the door it opened and her mother said, "My goodness, your arms must be breaking. Here let me help you."

"I thought maybe you'd be gone," Mindy said.

"No," her mother answered. "I'm staying home

tonight." She unwrapped the roses, looked quickly at Mindy, then turned away. Her slender shoulders sagged.

"It was Daddy's idea to bring them," Mindy said. "The vegetables, too."

"It seems strange that he'd go to the bother of making a garden," her mother said. "I mean, with only one there. And he never did like gardening."

"Well, I understand. Or I think I do," Mindy said. "He just wants things to be like they used to be. Even the night light."

Her mother didn't ask what she meant. *She knows.*

After the roses were arranged and the vegetables stored in the crisper compartment Mindy's mother asked, "Anything new going on in Oakville?"

*She's never asked before.* "No," Mindy said aloud. "Just the same good things — good to me, I mean."

"I just happened to be standing at the window when you drove up," her mother said. "Your father doesn't look quite as thin — as — when I happened to be looking out the last time."

"I noticed," Mindy said. "And I'm glad." There was a lot more she could have added. Like the news of the tape center at the store and her father's volunteer work. *But she wouldn't care.*

"There is one different thing — from last week," Mindy said, as she started to her room. "The canning factory opened." That was a safe and impersonal bit of news.

Her mother smiled. "And the whole place is like a cooking kettle of tomatoes."

# 8

The next week didn't seem twelve days long to Mindy for two or three reasons. One was that her mother didn't go out with Brad or Callie or anyone. She worked later than usual, but stayed in the apartment at night.

On Monday and Tuesday Mindy worked on the embroidery on her blouse. She'd decided to wear it to the ice-cream social with her navy linen skirt. The red organdy aprons Judy's mother was making for the waitresses would accent the tiny cardinals in the design.

She pulled her portable record player out of the closet and played it more than she had since leaving home. Somehow music made by someone else hadn't reached her — hadn't been comforting. Playing the piano had helped more — made a little more harmony — involved her in the melody.

She stayed in the apartment until Tuesday afternoon. Monday's thunderstorm had canceled her plan to go to the library. The last stitch of the Swedish needlework was anchored in the white blouse at three o'clock. Mindy pressed it and hung it in the closet.

The humidity of the July day made her feel sticky, and her hair clung to her forehead. Some days the clattering air conditioner couldn't cope with the heat of summer in Indiana.

Mindy decided to go to the park, then on to the library. She had two chapters to read in one book.

No one was sitting on the green park benches. Two little boys were passing a big beach ball back and forth. A lady was pushing a baby carriage along the winding walks. The leaves of the trees seemed limp and lifeless. There was no breeze.

As Mindy closed her book she glanced up to see a girl on the facing bench across the walk. Actually she wasn't sure it was a girl until she noticed the green eyeshadow and the shocking pink lipstick. Some boys wore hair to their shoulders and cut off jeans and oversize sweat shirts.

"Hi," Mindy said.

The thin-faced girl gave a quick little salute. "Is that your thing," she asked, "reading, I mean?"

"Sometimes," Mindy answered. "Do you like books?"

"I did," the girl said. "Way back when I didn't

see how the world really is."

"Oh?" Mindy said. She wasn't sure she wanted this conversation to be any longer.

"You live around here?" the girl asked.

"Back that way in an apartment."

"You mean the cells," the girl said. "Where people are stacked in rows."

Mindy smiled. "Maybe you *could* call them that — but cells don't usually have three rooms. I'm Mindy Porter."

The girl hesitated before answering. "I didn't mean for us to get involved in some kind of a relationship — a tangle or anything."

"Well, exchanging names isn't exactly tying a knot," Mindy said.

"I suppose you're right." I'm Lexie."

"Do you live around here?" Mindy asked.

"No," Lexie said. "I'm on my one-twelfth."

"Your what?"

"Oh, you know! Eleven months with my mother, one with my dad. I'm one of the fractioned kids of this stinking world. How about you?"

"If you mean are my parents divorced, the answer is yes. But I go home every week. And weeks at Christmas, Easter, and spring vacation."

"Where's home?"

Mindy answered truthfully. "I guess I should call the apartment home but it isn't. I'm still clinging to the place where I grew up — a little town south of here — called Oakville. I've only been here a few weeks — since school was out."

"Well. It's a rough scene at first," Lexie said. "I kept hoping that something good would happen. But

56

*Mindy and Lexie — two of the fractioned kids*

it didn't. So I caught on — learned how to work the system."

"I don't know what you mean."

"It's simple," Lexie said. "I tell each parent how bad the other is — you know — how stingy and cruel. And they fall into my trap. Do anything I want — to prove how much greater they are."

Mindy was shocked at first. Then she looked into Lexie's eyes. *She doesn't look like someone who's getting everything she wants. She looks lost and lonely.*

Mindy looked at her watch. "I'd better get to the library, then back to get dinner."

"You have to cook?"

"Sure. My mother works in a beauty shop. But I've always cooked — even at home. I like to, I guess."

Lexie shrugged her thin shoulders. "Me — I can't do anything. No need. My family's soaked in money. Dad runs that nightclub up the street, The Crazy Zebra. He lives in an apartment four floors up."

Mindy started to leave. Then she turned and said, "Maybe I'll see you again."

"Who knows?" Lexie said. "In this crazy world — who knows anything?"

Mindy felt a great sadness and a creeping fear. "Will I ever feel like Lexie does?" she thought. "Bitter, grasping, and hopeless?"

Later as she chopped leftover meat and vegetables into a casserole she examined her own thinking. Had she been selfish and considered only her own feelings? Did she dwell too much on how the divorce affected her? Had she expected her parents to give up a life that suited them in order to make her feel safe and happy?

Her mother called at five-fifteen saying she'd not be home until six. So Mindy waited to chop the pale green zucchini and dust it with cornmeal. It'd cook in butter while her mother showered.

Mindy walked to the piano and began playing the most restful of her favorite pieces while she waited. The liquid, flowing music of barcarole and the soothing Brahms *Lullaby*. Her neighbor surely couldn't object to such gentle vibrations.

By the time the casserole was bubbling and the squash was golden-crusted, her mother had changed into a pink linen shift. They were fixing trays to take to the cooler living room when the telephone rang.

Mindy answered, then turned and said, "Brad wants to talk to you."

She'd started to the kitchen when her mother said, "Don't go, Melinda. I *want* you to hear."

Mindy sank down on the end of the couch. Even one side of the conversation told her that something good could be happening.

"No, Brad," her mother said. "You are wasting your time and mine. There's no point in going on. I can't be what you expect."

After a pause Lila said. "Perhaps so. I'm sure I'm partly at fault for giving you the idea that I was all for fun and games. But not some games. So, good-bye."

Mindy picked up her fork and began to eat. She didn't really want to ask questions. What she'd heard was enough to make her feel good, better than she had for a long time.

Her mother sat down and began to sip iced tea. She'd brushed out her sculptured hairdo. Her face was framed in soft honey-colored waves.

"I'd rather not talk about that conversation — yet," she said. "OK?"

"I wasn't going to ask," Mindy said.

After the kitchen was in order Mindy's mother said, "I feel like taking a walk. But I guess it's not too safe after dark."

Mindy looked at her and bit her lip. *In Oakville it'd be OK.*

Callie called and Mindy heard her mother say. "You girls go on without me. I have some figuring to do and a letter to write."

Mindy went to sleep in the middle of one television show and woke up during another. She was trying to figure out what was happening when she realized that she was trying to match two separate plots.

She woke herself up getting ready for bed so she read a while. As she reached up to turn off the bed light, she saw that a lamp was still burning in the living room. She tiptoed out and saw that her mother was asleep.

As she went to the table she couldn't help but see the stamped letter. It was in the circle of light. It was addressed to Ruby Wheeler, Oakville, Indiana 47367.

"What's Mom writing to her about?" Mindy thought. "I don't think she has before."

She went back to her room but couldn't go to sleep. All sorts of thoughts bounced around in her mind. She thought of the girl named Lexie something or other who used her parents to get things which didn't seem to be making her very happy.

She went back over her mother's conversation with Callie and Brad, word by word, wondering if things were changing. *For the better? Or am I only hoping?*

9

By the time Friday came, Mindy felt a little divided in her feelings about leaving her mother alone for two whole days. She brought up the subject at breakfast. "What will you do?" she asked. "You and Callie have anything planned?"

"I don't know about Callie," her mother said. "But I have an idea I want to work on and it may take up most of Sunday."

"Anything I should know?"

"Yes, you should. But not until it's a sure thing. Which it isn't." Then she seemed to change the subject. "What will you be doing on Sunday? Has Judy said.

"No," Mindy answered. "But I'd guess we'll go to church."

"Will you? No, I mustn't ask that."

"You might as well," Mindy said. "Now that you've started."

"Well, I was wondering if the Rayburns would include your father in their plans for Sunday."

Mindy looked down at her toast and didn't answer for a while. She spread strawberry jam so thinly that it almost disappeared into the crust. "Would that be bad?"

"No. No," her mother said. "That's what I wanted to get said. I've been wrong trying to pin your visits to the pattern set by the judge. I know how you love your dad."

"And he loves me too, Mom."

"I know. I know."

Mindy cleaned the apartment and made a custard pie as a surprise for her mother. *She hasn't been eating much lately. She's almost as thin as Daddy.*

She was sprinkling flecks of nutmeg over the golden filling when her Aunt Eileen called from downtown Wayne City.

"We're heading for home in a couple hours," she said. "And I offered to be your bus driver. OK?"

"Great," Mindy said. "I'll be ready. But hold on a minute. Where are you?" She'd heard familiar background sounds. The whistling puffing of hair dryers, a mingling of voices, and the swish of running water.

"Oh, I'm at the Silver Brush," her Aunt Eileen said.

"You are!"

"Yes. You forgot to bring the straw bag my mother made for you. And besides, Sharon hasn't liked a single haircut since her Aunt Lila left Oakville."

"Oh," Mindy said. Her aunt sounded casual and what she said seemed reasonable. *But it still is a change. She and Mom have been mad at each other for months.*

By the time she reached Oakville she'd cleared her thoughts of most of the sad feelings which had clouded it for so long. She and her father stayed at home the early part of Friday evening. He'd brought a portable television home from the shop. "It's for a lady who lives out in the country alone," he said. "I thought we'd deliver it after we eat if you don't have anything else in mind."

"I'd like to go," Mindy said.

"Fine. We might even circle around and go to see your grandparents."

They didn't get back to Oakville until nearly ten. On the way home Mindy said, "Grandmother's so wonderful. Every single time I see her she's enthusiastic about something."

"True," her father said. "This world could use more like her."

The night breeze was cool on Mindy's cheek. Golden stars punctuated the deep blue sky. Suddenly she asked, "Daddy, how well did you know my other grandmother?"

Her father didn't speak for what seemed like a long time. *Is this a painful subject? Should I have asked?*

"Pretty well," her father said. "We had to go out there a lot because she was sick so much. Why? Don't

64

you remember her? You should."

"Oh, yes. I remember her," Mindy said. "But she always seemed so *old* — much more than Gram Porter does now."

"True," her father said. "It's a matter of thought, I guess. My mother's mind is busy with lively things."

Mindy leaned her head against the side of the car. Did she dare talk about her mother's fear of getting old? Or was this one of those times when what she might say would seem disloyal. *But Daddy surely knows.*

She also wished she could tell that there'd been a change in the situation in the apartment — that her mother wasn't seeing Brad or going out with the other operators. But it wasn't easy to mention Brad. She never had.

Saturday was crammed with activity. Judy and Mindy cut armfuls of flowers from their backyards and gardens, ragged robins, button zinnias, and delicate California poppies in soft shades of pink, blue, and lavender. They carried them to the church and arranged them in assorted vases.

Two men were setting up trestle tables on the grassy yard at the side. Another was stringing lights from one tree to the other. Mindy's father came over at noon to help. Then he and Mindy went home to eat bacon, lettuce, and tomato sandwiches with baked macaroni and cheese the oven had kept warm.

There was time for a swim that afternoon before the hour set for serving. Mindy had gone to these ice-cream socials for as long as she could remember. She'd sat on the folding chairs when her feet were at various distances from the grassy mat of the lawn. Every year she found it hard to choose between her Aunt Eileen's black walnut cake and her mother's chocolate fudge. But this year there was no such choice to make.

Judy, Mindy, and the other eight girls in the Dorcas Junior Sunday School Class took orders and carried plates of ice cream and cake on black enamel trays. The ties on their crisp organdy aprons fluttered and curled in the evening breeze.

The string of lights cast wavering shadows over the tables which were spread with grayish newsprint from the *Oakville Herald,* the weekly newspaper. Children ran around the church and played hide-and-seek behind the barberry bushes and the tall trees.

Mindy saw her father come down the cinder alley and cross the street. He looked nice in his white shirt and new charcoal slacks. She stopped at the end of the outside table and watched.

Her father looked toward the place where the Rayburns and his sister and her husband sat. Then he turned and walked to a place at the end. He sat down with Arthur Fenway whose wife had died four years ago and Rob Carstairs who'd never married.

A tight feeling came to Mindy's throat. She hurried over to Judy and said, "Have you eaten yet?"

"No," Judy said. "Why? Are you hungry?"

"Well, no. Not really," Mindy said. "But Daddy's here and I'd like to eat with him."

Judy looked up and down the tables. "There is

sort of a letup now. Care if I come along?"

"Naturally not!"

Mindy's father smiled as the girls sat down across from him and set their crinkled paper plates on the table. "Couldn't you find anyone nearer your age?" he said.

"Look around, Mr. Porter," Judy said. "Do you see any boys our age sitting down. They're either waiting in the shadows or sitting in cars."

"Except Kip," Mindy said. "He's dipping ice cream."

"I guess you're right," Mindy's father said. "I can — believe this or not — remember when I was that age. I wouldn't come out in front of the whole town in these bright lights and sit or talk with a girl."

"I suppose boys have been just plain chicken for a long time," Judy said.

"But they get over it," Mindy's father said. "Give them time."

"What *else* can we do?" Judy said.

It was ten o'clock before people began to wander away from the churchyard. Mindy's Aunt Eileen asked the Porters to ride home with them. Mindy decided to walk home with Kip to get her overnight bag. He'd waited patiently while she helped roll up the papers and empty vases.

The moon was a tissue paper disk in a deep blue sky. The fragrance of honeysuckle vines filled the misty air. The hollow call of a rain crow came from the grove beyond the edge of town. Mindy had often wondered why this bird had such a name. Its throaty calls could be heard on nights like this when the sky was dotted with gold and glinting stars.

"So you're staying all night," Kip said.

"Yes," Mindy said, "and all day tomorrow."

"Good."

Neither said a word until they came to the place where a tree overhung the sidewalk. "Be careful," Kip said. "The roots make a hump here."

"I know," Mindy said. "I know every one."

"You *could* have forgotten," Kip said.

"No," Mindy said. "I never could. It's like a map printed on my mind."

They sat on the patio and talked a while before going back up the street, until the air became suddenly chilly. Someone's radio was playing across the street. Dreamy Hawaiian music seemed to fit the moonlight, soft breezes, and fragrances of the night.

# 10

Judy and Mindy didn't have to be told to quit chattering and go to sleep. They were tired and besides they'd be together another day.

Everyone in the Rayburn house slept late the next morning. No one lingered over breakfast. If they did, they'd be late for church.

Judy's mother was on the telephone as the girls came down the stairs. She finished the conversation by saying, "Well, all right! You may bring fruit — if you insist."

Then she smiled at Mindy and said, "That was your father. We're having a backyard cookout at noon."

"And he's coming," Mindy said. "I'm glad."

Mrs. Rayburn bit her lip then she said, "We all try to include him in our activities — like before. Some even try matchmaking."

"But he's not interested."

"No," Mrs. Rayburn said, "Not at all."

Mindy could almost read Judy's mother's mind. *She's wondering if Mom goes out with anyone.*

She found herself saying, "Mother did see some-one. But she hasn't lately." She didn't say that it had only been a week since Brad had come to the apart-ment. *I guess I want to make things sound good — as good as possible.*

The church seemed cool after walking four blocks in the bright and silvery sunshine. The lovely stained-glass windows kept out some of the heat and the brilliance.

The organist was playing *Blessed Assurance.* Mindy glanced at the pew where she and her parents al-ways sat. "Daddy's here," she whispered.

"He said he was coming," Mrs. Rayburn said. "Be-cause you were here."

"Is it OK if I sit with him?"

"Certainly."

Mindy's father smiled as she sat down beside him. She loved the way his mouth turned up at one cor-ner when something pleased him.

After the responsive reading the chorister an-nounced the second song "Stand up for Jesus," but she didn't indicate that the congregation should rise to their feet. Mindy glanced at her father and he smiled at her. They were thinking the same thing re-membering the same words. Her mother always said

70

it was contrary to the spirit of the song to sing it sitting down.

It was good to be in a Sunday school class again. *Especially in my class.* She loved the way Judy's father read the Bible verses. He was an English teacher and often stopped to discuss the beautiful language of the Bible.

After church people stood around outside talking. They didn't do this too much in the sanctuary. It was a place apart for almost everyone. And catching up on the news and the crops and the state of the nation was done either in the basement or under the trees.

Judy's grandmother came over for a visit that day. Mindy had the feeling Mrs. Rayburn had invited her so that her father wouldn't feel out of place as he would've with two couples. The men broiled hamburgers on the grate of the stone fireplace in the corner of the yard. The girls helped carry out food and plates and the silverware.

Later in the afternoon Kip came over and brought his cousin Dave from Mt. Summit. The four young people took turns on the crank of the ice-cream freezer. They quit when it came to a grinding stop.

"Do we have any ice-cream cones?" Judy asked. "I'm in the mood for a triple dipper."

"Well," her mother said. "You'll have to run up to the drugstore."

"Is it open on Sunday now?" Judy's grandmother asked.

"Just an hour," Judy said. "From three to four for emergency prescriptions. Want to go, Mindy?"

71

"Sure. I'll go," Mindy said. "How about you boys?"

"We were about to start a volleyball game," Kip said. "Any objections?"

"None," Mindy said. "If you prefer batting a ball on a sticky afternoon that just shows —"

"Shows what?" Kip teased.

"Oh, I don't *know*," Mindy admitted. "That you prefer batting a ball, I guess."

As the girls started across the street, Judy said, "Let's go past the school. They were to work on the tennis courts this weekend and I've been too rushed to check."

"Do we have time?" Mindy asked. "I mean before the drugstore closes?" She was thinking that it wouldn't be much more than an hour before the Rayburns should be taking her back to Wayne City. *Or do they have to obey the judge?*

"There's time," Judy said. "It's only three-fifteen or maybe a little past."

The girls circled the school buildings and saw that four people were playing on the newly graded rectangle. As they headed west a car crossed Main Street at the intersection half a block away.

"Who was that?" Mindy asked. "Did you see?"

"Sure," Judy said. "Ruby Wheeler. Or didn't you know her in her yellow car?"

"I knew Ruby," Mindy said. "I meant the other one."

"I didn't notice," Judy said.

Mindy was puzzled at her own thinking. *Why would I get the idea that Mom would be in Oakville? But it looked a lot like her — from what little I could see. But a lot of people wore their hair in upsweep with curls on top. It was silly to think it was Mom.*

By the time five o'clock came the fresh peach ice cream was gone. Kip and David left soon after the tall can was empty. Mindy and Judy's father said it was time to get ready for Men's Fellowship meeting.

"So I guess it's good-bye time again, Daddy," Mindy said. "Until Friday."

"Until Friday," her father said rubbing his knuckles up and down one of her cheeks. "I'll be there."

The girls didn't talk much on the way to the city and Mrs. Rayburn was occupied with driving through Sunday evening traffic. As they passed the city limits Judy asked, "What do you have planned for this week? Anything special?"

"Nothing," Mindy said. "Nothing special or otherwise. I keep thinking I ought to get involved. But I don't know where to begin."

They came to a stoplight and Judy's mother said, "There's surely some way — some place — where you could meet friends, people your age."

"I suppose so," Mindy said. "There's a church across the park. I've thought of going. But to tell the truth I don't want to belong here. My place is back there. Maybe I'm just being stubborn. Dragging my feet as Grandpa Porter would say."

The light turned green and the car made the seven blocks to the apartment house just as the streetlights began to glow.

"Want to come up?" Mindy asked.

Mrs. Rayburn started to say no as Mindy expected. Then she said, "Yes, I think we will for a minute. Is it all right to park here?"

"You'd better pull around to the back — under the canopy," Mindy said. "There's a fifteen-minute limit here."

Mindy's mother was at home but she was dressed in a turquoise linen shift and beige pumps. "You going out, Lila?" Mrs. Rayburn said. "I wouldn't want to keep you."

"Oh, no," Mindy's mother said. "I was out for a while. On business."

Mindy looked at her mother's eyes. They were bright. *Business on Sunday?* She was even more puzzled when her mother insisted that Judy and Mrs. Rayburn stay for a tuna fish and lettuce sandwich. She talked and asked questions while she made lemonade and crushed ice.

"Mom hasn't been this friendly to anyone in Oakville since we left," Mindy thought. "Or for a long time before!"

Callie called before the Rayburns left. Mindy could hear parts of the conversation from the chair at the end of the kitchen table.

"No, Callie, no," her mother said. "I've decided. No, there's no point — I've done my thinking. Well, I'll see you tomorrow."

After the visitors left, Mindy's mother turned to her and said, "Are you awfully tired, Melinda?"

"No, Mom. Why? Are we going —"

"No, no, not tonight. But I have something to tell you. Let's go in where it's a little cooler."

74

# 11

A mixture of thoughts circled in Mindy's mind as she curled up on the end of the couch. She tried to piece things together to make a pleasant picture. Her mother had stayed in the apartment when she wasn't working. She'd *sounded* as if she didn't intend to see Brad anymore. She cautioned herself, "But maybe I'm building my hopes on hope."

Her mother turned the air-conditioner on low speed so that its clacking became a now-and-then clatter. She kicked off her shoes and sank down in the modernistic chair. She rubbed one cheek with a forefinger. "She doesn't know how to begin," Mindy thought. "Is that a bad sign?"

"Well," her mother said, drawing a deep breath. "I might as well jump in. How would you like the idea of moving back to Oakville?"

"How do you *think* I'd like it?" Mindy said. "But I don't understand. You don't mean back — "

"With your father. No, that's not a part of this move," her mother said. "But I've finally faced up to the fact that making a sharp break was a mistake in more than one way."

She went on to explain that she wasn't able to make as much money in the Silver Brush as she'd expected. The charges to customers were higher but the share paid to operators was on a lower scale.

"Also," she said. "I didn't realize how much it would cost us to live here — the rent, no garden, bus fare, and everything added up. In Oakville we could walk to any place we needed to go."

"But Daddy offered you a share — "

"Yes, he was more generous than you probably realize," her mother said. "But his long illness had put him in debt and I know he was just now getting the business on a sound basis. Besides, he pays your expenses — plus extras. But I am still not able to keep up. I did better when I was working for Ruby."

Things began to click into place in Mindy's mind. The letter to Ruby, the glimpse of someone in her car. "So you *were* in Oakville today," she said.

"Did you see me?" her mother asked. "I wonder how many other people did? But I'll have to get used to stares and whispers. I asked for them."

"But where will we live? When — "

"Well, I wrote to Ruby last week and she called

76

soon after I got home Friday night. It seems that I couldn't have approached her at a better time."

Mindy's mother went on to tell that Mrs. Wheeler was wanting to go to California to see her first grandchild. She didn't feel that she could afford to close up shop for a long stay but neither did she want to make the long trip for a few days' visit.

"So," Mindy's mother said, "Since I'll be the only operator in Oakville for a few weeks people will, we hope, rise above their resentment and come to me. So I can get at least some of my old customers back."

"Do you think everyone resents you?" Mindy asked. "I mean no one acts differently toward me."

"I should hope not," her mother said. "But with me it's not the same. Your father, he's well thought of. And it's only natural for people to take sides with him — against me for leaving."

Mindy didn't know what to say. It seemed sad, as it had many times before, that you couldn't come right out and express your true feelings especially with people you loved most. *But Mom's never told me why she wanted a divorce. Will she ever? And I can't talk about taking sides.*

"But going back," her mother said. "Ruby wants to leave in two weeks, the seventh of August. And that'll work out fine, since I'm supposed to give two weeks' notice at the shop here and our rent's paid to the tenth."

"Then I'll be home before school starts," Mindy said. She felt warm tears in her eyes. This was almost too good to be true. She'd about made up her mind to do anything possible in order to go back to

77

Oakville in the fall. But she hadn't expected it to be easy and hadn't been at all sure things would work out as she hoped. Then one of the questions which were circling in her mind popped out in words, "Where will we live? You didn't say."

"I didn't, did I?" her mother said. "Ruby's made her upstairs into a three-room apartment. She'd thought of moving into it and renting the downstairs. But she's lived in that big old house so long and accumulated so many pieces of antique furniture, she can't bear to part with what wouldn't go into three rooms."

"We don't have any furniture — except the piano," Mindy said. "Unless —"

"Unless I take some from home? Is that what you were going to say?"

"Yes, Daddy offered."

"I know," her mother said. "But I'm not ready to make that move. Not yet." She looked at her watch and said, "Do you know what time it is? Eleven-thirty. We'd better get to bed."

"I'm not one bit sleepy," Mindy said.

Her mother walked to the kitchen. Mindy heard the swish of running water and the clink of glass on the sink. She waited.

"Mom," she said as her mother came back into the living room. "I have to ask no matter how late it is. Are you doing this — moving back — just for me?"

Her mother walked over and cupped Mindy's face with her hands. "Partly, yes. I hadn't realized — and I should have — how deep your roots were. But there's more. I'm just not ready to talk about it yet."

78

"OK," Mindy said. "Moving back is so — well — thank you, Mom."

"Oh, Melinda," her mother said. Tears were streaming down her face. "How can you thank *me*?"

Mindy didn't go to sleep for a long time. She thought of the things she'd like to do even if it was the middle of the night. *I'd like to call Daddy and Judy and Gram and begin to pack so as to get out of this place in a rush. And I'd like to see Ruby's apartment.*

After the excitement faded to the back of her mind Mindy's sleep was deep. She was aware that morning came and that her mother said good-bye before she left for work, but she wasn't really awake until the telephone rang. She glanced at the clock as she hurried out to answer. *Ten o'clock already.*

"Mindy," her Aunt Eileen said. "I began to think you weren't going to answer."

"I overslept," Mindy said. "Maybe I didn't hear all the rings."

"No matter," her aunt said. "I'm really calling for your father."

"Is something wrong?"

"No, no. But your grandmother's been wanting to go to Iowa to see her cousin and she intended to drive. But we'd rather she didn't. So Jay's taking her out and they'll be gone until Thursday."

"This is sort of sudden, isn't it?" Mindy asked. "I mean, Daddy didn't say anything yesterday."

"I know," her aunt said. "But you know my mother! She's the one who had the sudden notion. We found out what she was thinking last night. It took your father a while to talk her into changing

79

her mind, and make his own plans. Then, he couldn't get a call through to you."

"I know, there are party lines in the city, too," Mindy said.

"Well — that's all I have to say. Your dad will be there to get you as usual Friday. I wouldn't be too surprised if he doesn't call from Iowa."

Mindy was disappointed at first. She'd meant to call her father first thing and tell him they were moving back. She'd had the impulse to tell her aunt but wanted her father to be the first to know.

As she scrubbed her face and dressed she decided perhaps things were working out for the best. "I'd like to see Daddy's face when he hears the news. That's worth waiting for."

# 12

Mindy went to the kitchen to fix breakfast for herself. She was hungrier than she'd been for a long time. She poured cereal out into a bowl and slipped first one, then another piece of bread into the slots of the toaster.

"What am I going to do with myself all this week — and then the next? All this happiness ought to be put into use." She looked around the small kitchen. "If I know Mom, she'll want to leave this place clean. I'll wash these walls whether they need it or not."

A summer storm came up in the early afternoon. The sky became so overcast with smoky gray clouds that Mindy turned on all the lights in the kitchen and living room. Otherwise she couldn't see whether or not she was leaving streaked places.

Thunder rumbled as if the sky was a giant rolling roof, like the back porch on her grandparents' farm home. Flashes of lightning fired the windows. Then the rain began, first a patter, then a steadily increasing drumming. Mindy looked down on the street. There were no pedestrians and cars crept through the downpour, their headlights a snaky line of murky gold eyes.

Soon the air coming in the one kitchen window was cool and fresh. Mindy turned off the clattering air conditioner and opened the apartment to the natural refreshment of the rain-washed atmosphere.

Her mother called to be sure she was not out in the storm. "Did you call your father?" she asked.

"No," Mindy said. And after she explained she added, "But I wanted to."

When her mother heard that she'd been cleaning walls she said, "Well! That's very thoughtful of you. Just for that I'll take you out to eat."

"Great," Mindy said. "But won't it take too much money? I mean if we have so many expenses."

"We'll go to that little tearoom half a block down. Its prices are reasonable. Callie says their blueberry muffins are delicious. Be ready about six. OK?"

"OK," Mindy said.

She finished the kitchen as the rain stopped. After taking a shower she decided to dress and take a walk over to the park.

At first she thought she was going because she wanted to see it when the trees, grass, and benches weren't dust-coated. But as she wandered along the winding paths she realized she was looking for the girl named Lexie. She hadn't seen her since that one meeting. "She may have gone back to her mother. Her one-twelfth of a year visit with her father could be over."

The park benches were still wet so Mindy kept walking. There was no one in sight except a few people who were using the park as a shortcut to other places.

Mindy thought about Lexie as she went back toward the apartment. What would happen to her? She didn't seem to feel that she belonged any-where. "And she pretends not to care," Mindy thought. "That's sad — like living in emptiness."

The meal at the tearoom was a pleasant change. Wall lamps with apricot shades threw a half-moon of mellow light over the small tables which lined either side of the long room.

As Mindy buttered her berry muffin three people came to the table ahead of them, a couple near the age of her parents and a lady who was much older.

"Here, Grandmother," the younger woman said. "Is this table all right?"

"I'd say so," was the answer. "It seems to have the proper number of legs."

"Isn't she pretty?" Mindy whispered.

"You mean the one with the checked suit?"

"No — well, she *is*," Mindy said. "But I meant the other." She glanced up to meet her mother's eyes. They were clouded and sort of frightened.

Mindy suddenly wanted to bring something out in the open. If the hidden dread of being old had caused all this unhappiness, wasn't it time to talk about it?

"I think a lot of older people are lovely and great — like Gram Porter."

"Well — yes," her mother said slowly. "But not all of them. Not my mother. Or don't you remember her?"

"A little," Mindy said. "She always seemed the same to me — not young, or fun — "

"Just sick and old — and complaining. I had that picture in front of me all my life. It's horrible."

"But couldn't anyone be that way — if that's the way they chose?"

Her mother picked up her fork and cut a bite from her chicken pie. "I guess I supposed it was largely hereditary. I never thought you had a choice. Of course, your father tried — but I don't want to go into that now."

Mindy felt she'd come close to learning what had caused the final quarrel, the breakup. *But Mom backed away again. Yet I'm understanding more all the time.*

The apartment was cool enough for sound sleeping that night. "I *could* iron," Mindy's mother said. "But this night is made for catching up on sleep."

"I'll do the ironing tomorrow," Mindy said. "It'll help pass the time."

The next few days seemed to drag as much as usual but Mindy wasn't miserable and bored. She played the piano for hours when she knew the neighbor was away. She even dug out her finger exercise book. It wouldn't hurt to exercise. Maybe she could start taking lessons when they got home.

She got up early Friday morning to eat with her mother. "There's one thing I hope you'll have time to do for me," Mrs. Porter said. "Will you go ask Ruby if the circulars are printed?"

"Circulars?"

"Yes, she's mailing announcements to her customers and my old ones, about her absence and my return."

Mindy's knife clanked to her plate. "Oh, Mom. Do you suppose Ruby's telling people? Before Daddy finds out!"

"No. no. She wouldn't do that," her mother said. "I told her I'd let her know when to spread the news."

"Oh, good," Mindy said.

"You can hardly wait," her mother said. "I can tell. Your eyes are sparkling. Well, I must run. See you tomorrow night, Melinda."

Mindy followed her mother to the door. "Are you going to work late tonight?"

"Not unless we get some extra appointments. But I won't mind. And don't worry. I'll get inside before dark."

Mindy had her overnight bag packed by noon. And that turned out to be a wise move. Her father came to town early in order to pick up repair parts. He called from a pay telephone over on the four-lane highway. "I thought you might want to eat with me," he said. "Do you think it would be OK?"

"Yes. I'd like to, and I think it will. But Daddy, come up, will you? I have something important to tell you. Or is there time?"

"There's time," her father said, "for what you think's important."

Mindy's father had never been in the apartment but he didn't seem to pay any attention to the surroundings. He kept his eyes on her face.

"Sit down, Daddy," she said. "While I tell you this great and wonderful news." She sank down on the puffy black hassock facing him. "We're moving back to Oakville next weekend."

Her father shook his head as if to clear it of puzzled thoughts. "I don't understand — why — "

"Well, I don't think I really know the entire reason," Mindy said. But Mom says the income at the Silver Brush isn't what she expected. And it costs more to live here."

"But I offered — " her father said.

"I know. She told me," Mindy said. "But Daddy, don't, *please* don't, try to get her to take more money. I know there's a lot that I don't see, but I feel sure this move's *right*. Mom's more like she used to be."

Her father cleared his throat and said, "Well, I'd still like to help her. To let her know that her half of our family business will come her way when she says the word. No matter what it takes."

"I think she knows that."

"Well, anyway, I have to do this," her father said, getting to his feet. He walked to the telephone, dialed so rapidly there was a continual clicking. It was as if he'd secretly rehearsed the number. Mindy listened with her heart seeming to beat in her throat. It had been a long time since her parents had talked or even spoken to each other.

*Will Mom be angry — maybe hang up on him?*

"Mrs. Porter, please. Lila? Melinda's told me. And I want you to know I'll help you in any way possible. And one other thing. I realize how difficult it is for you — to go back. Well — so long."

Mindy watched her father's face. He was thoughtful but not exactly sad. "I'm bursting to know. What did she say?" Mindy asked.

"She thanked me and said she was expecting me to call. Now, are we ready to go?"

"We're ready!" Mindy said.

# 13

Mindy went to the wholesale and supply houses with her father. Somehow she felt her mother wouldn't object. But she did call to ask permission to leave for Oakville an hour and a half ahead of time.

"Daddy will wait if you say so," Mindy said.

"Well, that would be a little unreasonable," her mother said. "Not that I've never been guilty of that! So, run along. And have fun."

The twenty-six hours at home were almost like old times. The hours and the activities went together in kind of a harmony except for one thing. Her mother wasn't there. It was like a loved song played with only one hand.

Mindy had the feeling that she'd like to tell everyone immediately that she and her mother were moving back. "But Mom wouldn't like for the whole town to be gossiping all at once. But I *have* to tell some people like Gram Porter, Aunt Eileen, Kip, and Judy."

Her father let her out in front of the house, then went on to the store with the repair parts. The green lawn was clipped and the front walk had been scrubbed.

Mindy saw that the front door was open and she called through the screen mesh. "Yoo hoo. I'm here."

Her Aunt Eileen came through the long living room carrying a cloth and a spray can of window cleaner. "Well, hello there. You're early."

"I know," Mindy said. She looked around the room. It looked the same except for the space where her piano had set. The rose and beige slipcovers on the chairs were clean and straight. Rose corduroy pillows were plumped on the brown couch. A bouquet of pink Shasta daisies and fringed white zinnias were arranged in a turquoise pottery pitcher.

Mindy dropped down in the high-backed armchair. "Oh, this feels good," she said. "Home is all around me. Things look nice."

"Well, thank you, Melinda," her aunt said. "If I have a flair for anything it's for housekeeping."

"You really have it!" Mindy thought of her news. "Sit down please, if you're not in a rush."

"Well, my parents are coming in to eat with us, and you're invited too. But I have things under control. What's on your mind?"

"Something's happened," Mindy said. "This is my last weekend trip to Oakville."

"What?" her aunt said. "Why? Where?"

Mindy saw the hurt and confused look on her aunt's face. "Oh, Aunt Eileen. I said that all wrong. What I meant is we're moving back to Oakville. Next weekend. Isn't that fabulous?"

"Yes," her aunt said. "*That's* fabulous. For once you kids' extravagant language fits. But how —" Then she looked at the clock. I have to run home and get the chickens on to fry. Could you come along and tell me the whole story?"

"Sure!" Mindy said. "I'll run up and change and be at your back door in two shakes as Granddad says. Say, what does he mean by that?"

"Nothing that makes sense," her aunt said. "He used to say two shakes of a dead lamb's tail. I always wondered who'd want to shake the tail of a dead lamb or why. See you."

After the move was discussed, her aunt floured and browned the pieces of chicken and peeled potatoes. While they sizzled and sputtered in the heavy iron skillet Mindy called Judy.

When Mindy went back to the kitchen she spread the linen cloth on the extended table and set it with creamy china and bone-handled knives, forks, and spoons.

Her aunt was quiet for several minutes. She was sprinkling toasted coconut over the frosting on a three-layer cake. "You know, Melinda. I've always believed that your parents would resolve their differences some day."

"Believed, Aunt Eileen, or hoped?" Mindy asked.

"It's deeper than hope, more like faith," her aunt said. "I've thought of the Bible verse, 'Faith is the evidence of things not seen.' What's not seen is the character of Lila and Jay. And the strong good years of their marriage."

"You think coming back might be a step in that direction?" Mindy asked.

"Well," her aunt said. "It *not* a step away. That's for sure!"

Sharon came home from her swimming lesson and asked Mindy to go upstairs and see the dress she'd made in 4-H Club. Before they came down, their grandparents drove in from the farm. And Mindy hurried down to tell them the news.

"Sounds like Lila's getting her head back on her shoulders," Granddad Porter said.

"Now, Will," his wife said. "Be glad, not critical."

"Who says I'm not glad? I'm tickled pink."

The family gathering was a time of laughter and lighthearted conversation. Even Mindy's father was relaxed and in a teasing mood.

Everyone sat outside until after nine o'clock when Mindy's grandfather said, "Say, Elizabeth, I'm going to have to drive ninety miles an hour to get home by my bedtime."

"Why don't you stay all night?" Mindy's father asked.

"Please," Mindy begged. "We stayed with you last time."

After listening to a few more pleas Mr. Porter said, "Well, I reckon we could. That eighty acres will probably be there tomorrow. Don't know as it needs us to weigh it down."

Mindy didn't have a chance for a private conversation with her grandmother until the next morning. But she and her father did talk after the others had gone upstairs. She was putting some pieces of leftover chicken away when he came into the kitchen.

"Too sleepy to talk a while?" he asked.

"No," she said.

"Then let's go in where the chairs are comfortable."

"There's been something on my mind," her father said after she curled up on the couch. "It's taken me a long time to put shattered pieces together and see what I could've done to prevent this divorce."

"You — " Mindy said. "You never wanted it."

"True," her father said. "But I made a mistake when your mother took the path that led her farther away."

"You mean when she went to work in Wayne City?"

"Yes. And when staying late became an issue."

"I remember that," Mindy said. "I didn't like it either."

"Well, I suppose I felt that she was going too far away from her home too often — and from me. And I said the wrong thing. The worst possible."

"I don't understand."

"We had some lengthy arguments and I was scared at what I saw ahead. So I told her that she'd be happier if she didn't strain so hard to keep young. *And* that did it. That was the last argument."

"But I don't see that you said anything so terrible," Mindy said.

"To her it was," her father said. "She's had this fear — of aging early like her mother."

"I know," Mindy said.

"How, Melinda? How do you know?"

"Mom talked about it. One night last week."

"She did! That's good!" her father said. "She never has that I know of. Just kept it bottled up — a kind of inner panic or hysteria."

"That's sad," Mindy said. "And lonely."

"I know," her father said. "I should have seen her viewpoint. Realized that the image of mother to her and that of mine are as unlike as daylight and dark. Well. I'm glad she's coming back. I keep thinking how hard it must be for her to swallow her pride. I wish somehow I could make it easier."

Mindy got up and walked to her father's chair. She scratched his shoulder gently. "Oh, Daddy. You're so good. And do you know something? Maybe you've done more than you think — by keeping things as they were."

After Mindy went to bed she lay awake for several minutes. She could see the silvery crescent of the quarter moon above the house next door. Birds twittered a soft night song in the honeysuckle vine.

She examined her thinking as she'd done many times before? Am I selfish? Thinking about my own happiness? Is it wrong to be so happy if this move's hard on Mom's pride?

Things really get mixed up. People hurting others because of penned up fears. Can things ever be right again? Then she thumped and doubled her pillow. *Don't be greedy, Melinda, and strain for the very best. Be glad for better.*

# 14

When Melinda began to come out of the deep and faraway place of sleep she heard a steady pounding. For a few seconds she thought she was back in the apartment. Her heart thudded with sudden fear. *Who can be at the door this time?*

Then the sounds of home quieted her heart — the twittering birds in the honeysuckle vine, and the sharp yap of the neighbors' Yorkshire terrier. But the pounding was unusual.

Mindy jumped out of bed and ran to the front window. No one was in sight. Then she ran to the one which overlooked the side porch. She caught a glimpse of two shoe soles to the left. She raised

the screen section and stuck her head out. "Granddad! What are you *doing?*"

Mr. Porter crooked his neck to look back at her.
"What does it look like I'm doing?"

"Fixing the roof," Mindy said.

"Right. Give one dozen Mars candy bars to the
young lady with the pink rollers in her hair."

Mindy smiled. Her grandfather was always sprinkling his conversation with lines from old radio and
newer television shows. She usually knew what they
meant, not from ever hearing the program but because her granddad used them so often.

"Well. Don't fall," she said.

"I never do. Do I?"

Mindy's grandmother was standing at the range
and turned to say, "What woke you, honey — your
tinkering granddad?"

"Maybe," Mindy said. "But it's time! Nine o'clock!
I don't like sleeping away my Saturdays. What are
you cooking anyway?"

"Oh," her grandmother said. "I saw this recipe
for beef stroganoff in a magazine this morning. And
I just had to try it."

"Gram! You've been making scrumptious
stroganoff for years and years!"

"Well. But this one's a little different," her
grandmother said. "It takes Romano cheese and a dash
of oregano."

"You don't fool me, not one little bit," Mindy said.
"You're just using any excuse to fix something for us
to eat which happens to be one of Daddy's favorites."

"Guilty," her grandmother said. "Now! What's on
your schedule today?"

"Actually," Mindy said. "I don't feel the same great strain to crowd everything into a few hours. Now that I know I'll be home all the time. But I'm supposed to go see Ruby Wheeler — for Mom."

"Are you going to look at the apartment?" Mrs. Porter asked.

"There's another reason, but I did think of asking," Mindy said. "Do you think it would be all right?"

"I'm sure it would. Ruby'd understand that you'd like to see where you're to live. In fact, I'd like to trot along."

"Good," Mindy said. "I'm for that."

"Well, we'd better dash. Your grandfather will be trying to drag me home as soon as those shingles are replaced. I'll set this oven — take off this apron — pick up this purse — and now I'm ready."

Ruby was in her beauty shop in a room at the end of her big square house. It had once been a sun porch and the heavy monk's cloth drapes were pulled to keep out the burning heat of the July day. The square room seemed dark until Mindy's eyes became adjusted. Then she saw that Ruby was cutting a little girl's hair.

"Hello there, ladies," Ruby said, looking over the silver rims of her glasses. "Are you customers, renters, or visitors?"

"I'd be a customer," Mindy's grandmother said. "If my husband wasn't pawing the ground to get home. But for now it's Mindy that has the business to transact."

Mindy told Mrs. Wheeler that her mother wanted to see the circulars if they were printed "and she says it's OK to mail or deliver them. I was wondering — would it be all right if we saw the apartment?"

"Sure thing!" Ruby said. "The key's on that hook under the mirror. Go right on up. May be a little stuffy up there — so open the windows."

A wide stairway led from the front hall to the second floor. They went in the long room which ran across the front of the house. "This is nicer than the place in the city," Mindy said. The furniture was a mixture of white wicker and wood with antiqued white finish. Cushions and lampshades of brown and bittersweet tied the pieces together.

The one bedroom was large and the room which had been converted into a kitchen covered almost as much space. "It is real cozy," Mindy's grandmother said. "But — "

"You still think we belong two blocks down the street," Mindy said. "So do I." She walked over and opened one half of the window. Traffic was heavier in Oakville on Saturday. Tires whirred and trucks chuffed as they pulled across intersections. But there wasn't so much noise that Mindy couldn't hear the chimes in the church tower or the sounds of children's voices on the sidewalk.

After looking at the old-fashioned brass bed and the claw-footed bathtub, Mindy and her grandmother left the key with Ruby and walked home.

They could see Mr. Porter standing on the front steps as they rounded the corner. "He's raring to go," Mindy's grandmother said. "And I suppose we should. But sometimes — "

"Sometimes what, Gram? Or should I ask?"

"Oh, I might as well say it. I often wondered if

97

I'm married to a farmer or a farm."

"You don't like living in the country?"

"Most of the time I do," her grandmother said. "But once in a while it doesn't seem that I have a choice and this makes me a little rebellious."

"That sounds like the women's liberation thing."

"Maybe. In a sense," her grandmother said. "I guess all of us would like to be liberated from something. But I have less than most. Far less. And I find ways of being myself without upsetting anyone too much."

After her grandparents left Mindy walked down to the store. She hadn't seen the new paint in the salesroom or the fenced off section of the long room called the *Tape Corner*.

Her father and his Saturday helper were busy and there seemed to be no let up in the stream of customers. Mindy walked to the cash register. "Why don't I go home and fix us a lunch? Would that help?"

"It sure would," her father. "Days like this don't happen often. If they did, I'd have to hire a clerk or cashier."

Mindy smiled and said, "How about me?"

Her father grinned. "You don't think I've overlooked that possibility, do you? We'll talk about it later."

Mindy stayed in the store for an hour and a half after they ate the sandwiches, fruit, and cookies. "I hope you can close in time for us to eat Gram's casserole before we leave," she said as she left.

"We will make a point of that," her father answered.

They had customers but they thinned out soon after two. That's when the little league play-offs began on the school baseball diamond. Mindy called Judy and the girls rode their bikes first to the school, then to see who was swimming.

Judy's mother had said she couldn't go in the water until she was over her cold and Mindy didn't feel in the mood to change and then change again.

The bicycle ride ended at Judy's home and the girls sat in the backyard and talked until nearly five.

Judy said that there was to be a new science teacher and a new librarian at school. Mindy asked how many were going to church camp.

The air was misty with humidity. The leaves on the trees quivered in the slight afternoon breeze.

For some reason Mindy thought of Lexie. "Do you remember that I said I hadn't met anyone near my age?"

"Yes."

"Well — I did later," Mindy said. "Only once and for a little while. But I keep thinking about her. She was so bitter and lonely and almost hard."

"Why?" Judy asked.

"Over her parents' divorce," Mindy said.

Neither girl spoke for a few minutes.

"But you aren't — bitter, I mean," Judy said.

"No. I guess not," Mindy said. "But I can see how Lexie — that was her name — felt. Sort of let down. I've never really said this out loud before, Judy, but I've often thought that if *my* parents loved me as much as I used to *think* they did, they'd have worked things out — somehow."

"Oh, Mindy! That's such a sad way to feel."

"I know."

Judy pushed the glider into a swinging motion. "But I've known one or two kids who were *glad* their parents got a divorce. It stopped fights."

"But mine didn't fight," Mindy said. "Not until a year and a half ago and then not often — at least not that I heard."

"There's another thing — well, I don't know how to say this," Judy added. "But no one thinks your father's to blame."

"I realize that," Mindy said. "So does Mom. That's why it's going to be hard on her to come back — to face people."

"Then why is she?"

"Well," Mindy said. "I know what she *says*. That living's cheaper here and that she didn't realize how miserable I'd be in Wayne City. I guess she thought I'd adjust — maybe because young people are supposed to be able to change."

"Sometimes I think grown-ups have terrible memories," Judy said. "All they'd have to do is look back, to see how important friends and home and feeling loved was to them."

The chimes in the church tower began to send a little melody of sound waves out over Oakville. Their vibrations were a part of home.

"I'd better run and warm up Grandmother's casserole," Mindy said. Judy walked to the front gate with her. "Just think," Mindy added," by this time next week I'll be here for good."

"I was thinking the very same thing," Judy said. "Mindy, do you think your parents will ever go back together?"

Mindy wasn't ready to express her true feelings. *Or am I afraid to hope?* She smiled at her friend, put her hands together in a prayerful position, and almost whispered one word, "Please."

# 15

Mindy and her mother spent most of Sunday exploring the city. They took a bus to the university area and explored the art gallery. "While we're here we might as well see it," Mrs. Porter said. As they wandered through the wide corridors of the arts building Mindy heard music.

"I wonder where," she said as she stopped to listen.

"It's coming from that wing of the building," her mother said. "Let's go see if we can find out what's going on." A few people were hurrying through heavy doors with diamond-shaped panes of glass.

Mindy pointed to a poster on what looked like an

artist's easel. The words, "Presenting Rosemary Grace Miller in her Graduate Recital" were printed in gold letters.

"Do you suppose we'd have to pay?" Mindy asked.

"I don't think so," her mother said. "No one's taking money or tickets. Want to go in?"

"Oh, yes," Mindy said.

They sat at the back so as not to disturb the listeners or the musicians.

The garnet-colored curtains were pulled back almost all the way and hung in rippled folds. A grand piano sat sidewise in the center of the stage. A girl in a long white dress trimmed with shining crystal beads sat on the padded bench.

She played five selections. Mindy knew the names of some and wished she knew the others. *I'll look around for a program as we leave.*

She drew a deep breath as they walked out into the bright sunlight. "Oh, Mother. Wasn't she wonderful?"

"Yes," her mother said. "I guess I didn't realize that graduates of the music department were so professional."

"That's what I want to do. Come here to school — be a music major."

Her mother smiled. "Are you old enough to be sure this time?"

"I think so," Mindy said as they walked toward the bus stop. "It seems right. Most of the things I've talked about doing were because of books I've read. You know, a nurse and medical missionary and ballet dancer. But this, well, it's connected with something I love and a deep down feeling."

Callie came up to the apartment soon after they returned, but she didn't stay long. She asked Lila Porter, then Mindy, to go riding with her and another operator. "We got no place special in mind. Just drive around. See if there's any interesting action to be found."

"No, thank you," Mindy's mother said. "I'd planned to make lists of the things at the Silver Brush which are mine."

After Callie left Mindy asked, "How old is Callie?"

"I'm not sure, why?"

"Oh, I just wondered," Mindy said. "You can't tell. I mean she's attractive — in a way. But her makeup's like — "

"A mask?"

"Yes. I guess that's what I was thinking," Mindy said.

"And so is all the dashing and rushing to have fun. Driving around from one drive-in to another like teenagers. I was always aware of this — even when I was in the car — and pretending to be having a good time."

Mindy wanted to say something to keep the conversation going. But she was afraid she'd choose the wrong words. She picked up a book and her mother sat down with a pad of yellow paper. Neither spoke for several minutes. The ball-point pen squeaked on the paper and the pages of Mindy's book whispered as they were turned.

"You know," Mindy's mother said. "I've been thinking about Callie and her friends. And somehow she's opened my eyes. Growing old frightened me so long — seemed so terrible. But there comes a time when some things should be out-grown. And that's good."

Mindy smiled and drew a deep breath. Was this something her mother had needed to realize for years and years? *I never thought that grown-ups had to keep on working at this thing called maturity.*

Mindy began packing the next morning and by Wednesday evening her mother said they were down to one table setting, one pan, one change of clothing. It wasn't quite that way but boxes were stacked in three corners of the apartment.

"I didn't realize we'd brought or accumulated so much," Mindy's mother said as she finished scrubbing the kitchen floor for the last time.

"I know," Mindy said. "And I was wondering how are we going to get all this stuff to Oakville?"

"Well, I called a trucking company," her mother said. "To get prices and are they high! Then Ruby called me at work and said she had the services of a van. It will be here at six o'clock Friday evening."

"Does she own one?"

"No, I don't think so. She wasn't quite clear," Mindy's mother said. "Anyway she said the vehicle was big enough for your piano and dozens of boxes."

By the time her mother came home on Friday evening Mindy had looked out the window several times. As the time of leaving came nearer, the more impatient she became. She didn't really think anything had gone wrong. She just wanted to get away.

"I fixed tuna sandwiches," Mindy said. "Before I packed the fresh food in the ice chest. Want one?"

"Yes," her mother said. "I'll eat one as I change and pack these clothes."

Mindy took a paper cup of iced tea and stood at the window.

The evening traffic was heavy and noisy and the red light at the intersection held back a line half a block long. As Mindy watched a gleaming white truck edged to the curb. Her breath caught in her throat as she read the words *Porters, Oakville,* which were written in red script on the side.

"That's Daddy. He has a new van! Is he — " She started to tell her mother who'd come to move them. Then she hesitated. *Mom won't like this.* But as she watched two young men came across the sidewalk. *They're Kip's brothers. Daddy's sent them. He thought Mom wouldn't want him to come. Or would she?*

The van was loaded before seven o'clock. Mindy had assumed that she and her mother would ride in the truck. As Kip's oldest brother picked up the last carton he said, "Say! It slipped my mind but Mrs. Wheeler's coming for you two any time now."

"Well, that's nice of her," Mindy's mother said. "But we could have ridden in the truck."

It was dark by the time they reached Oakville. The van was almost unloaded and Mindy and her mother concentrated on making the bed and the couch for sleeping.

Ruby went downstairs to finish packing. She was planning to head west when her last customer walked out of the shop the next afternoon.

It was after nine o'clock before Mindy and her mother felt they could sit down and relax. "It looks cozy and restful," Mrs. Porter said.

Mindy was thinking about going to bed when a startling thought popped into her mind. "Mom! It's

106

Friday. I'm supposed to go home — to be with Daddy."

Her mother clapped the palm of her hand to her forehead. "I didn't think of that! Of course Jay knew we'd be moving — it's his truck. But is he expecting you?"

"Well, I don't know," Mindy said. But she was thinking, *Mom hasn't said Daddy's name for months. He's been "your father."* "What should I do?"

"You should at least go down and talk to him. Tell him we're here. Then stay if you like. That was the judge's decision."

Mindy stopped in the doorway. "You know something, Mom! I find it hard not to hate that man! That judge, I mean."

"Why in the world — "

"Because," Mindy said. "What right does he have to divide me — or anyone up like — furniture or money."

"You sound quite positive. Have you felt this way the whole time?"

"Yes!" Mindy said.

"But you never said — "

"No one asked me," Mindy said. "At least not for a long time. Well — I'll see you later."

Lights were on in three of the rooms of Mindy's home and the square-sided lantern on the iron post threw a golden circle on the lawn. She hurried up the steps and nearly ran into her father.

"Well, I'm home," she said.

"I know," her father said. "I drove past and saw the unloading. Is the apartment in order — fit to live in?"

107

"Yes," Mindy said. "Of course there's unpacking to do. It's a lot nicer than that place in Wayne City. But not as good as this. No place ever could be!"

"You're staying?"

"Mom said it would be OK. That it was the agreement."

"Hungry?" her father asked.

"Yes, I am. It has been hours since I ate, at least it seems like it. What's here?"

"Well, we could have ice-cream floats and your Aunt Eileen sent over some brownies."

"Yum, yum!"

As Mindy poured orange juice over scoops of ice cream she said, "Daddy, do I have to obey that court decision now? I mean, am I to come here only on Friday and until Saturday?"

"I hope not," her father said. "I've been thinking about this too. And I've made up my mind to try to get your mother to sit down and talk. About this and other things. Think she will?"

"Maybe," Mindy said. "She *did* appreciate having the truck move us. And she called you Jay."

"Is that a good sign?" her father asked. "What has she called me — or do I want to know?"

Mindy smiled. "Nothing terrible. Unless you call being labeled as 'my father' something bad."

She took time to call Judy before she went up to her room.

She was tired and things were sort of jumbled in her mind like the tape on a recorder when it became twisted and wrinkled. She knew what had already happened. They were back in Oakville. Her mother gave hints that she'd been wrong in moving. But

108

does that mean she's sorry she divorced Daddy? Mindy thought. And does moving to Oakville mean that the next step will bring us all together?

She crawled into bed and thought of everyone in her family, everyone who'd been sad and hurt. It's so easy for people to make such big mistakes. People like Mom who's not mean or wild or anything. Just scared about getting old and wanting to grab at youth and fun.

Mindy thumped her pillow into fluffiness and snuggled under the crisp sheet. "It sure gives us kids a lot to think about — especially if we're divided by divorce."

But somehow she wasn't sad. It was like a hurt was healing. Or like wrong notes in a song were being eliminated. *Maybe life will be more like music for me someday. Some of the time anyway.*

*Jerry Burney photo*

# The Author

Dorothy Hamilton was born in Delaware County, Indiana, where she still lives. She received her elementary and secondary education in the schools of Cowan and Muncie, Indiana. She attended Ball State University, Muncie, and has taken work by correspondence from Indiana University, Bloomington, Indiana. She has attended professional writing courses, first as a student and later as an instructor.

Mrs. Hamilton grew up in the Methodist Church and participated in numerous school, community, and church activities until the youngest of her seven children was married.

Then she felt led to become a private tutor. This service has become a mission of love. Several hundred girls and boys have come to Mrs. Hamilton for gentle encouragement, for renewal of self-esteem, and to learn to work.

The experiences of motherhood and tutoring have inspired Mrs. Hamilton in much of her writing.

Seven of her short stories have appeared in quarterlies and one was nominated for the American Literary Anthology.

Since 1967 she has had fifty serials published, more than four dozen short stories, and several articles in religious magazines. She has also written for radio and newspapers.

Mrs. Hamilton is author of *Anita's Choice, Christmas for Holly, Charco, The Killdeer, Tony Savala, Jim Musco, Settled Furrows, Kerry, The Blue Caboose, Mindy, The Quail, Jason, The Gift of a Home, The Eagle, Cricket, Neva's Patchwork Pillow, Linda's Raintree,* and *The Castle.*